SAPTARSHIS

H.A. Padmini is a software professional dabbling in writing. Born and brought up in Hyderabad, Padmini is an alumna of University College of Engineering, Osmania University. Keenly interested in writing since childhood, she has published quizzes, articles and stories. A collection of short stories for children, *Tales of Anantha Bhargava Somayaji*, was her first published work. This is her second book on Indian mythology.

Padmini loves to take out time for watching movies, travelling and reading. She resides in Bangalore with her parents. She welcomes feedback and discussions on her works at hapadmini@hotmail.com.

Also by the author

Mahabharata and the Marvellous Cycle of Boons, Curses and Vows

SAPTARSHIS

H.A. Padmini

Published by
Rupa Publications India Pvt. Ltd 2021
7/16, Ansari Road, Daryaganj
New Delhi 110002

Sales centres:
Allahabad Bengaluru Chennai
Hyderabad Jaipur Kathmandu
Kolkata Mumbai

Copyright © H.A. Padmini 2021

All rights reserved.

No part of this publication may be reproduced, transmitted, or stored in a retrieval system, in any form or by any means, electronic, mechanical, photocopying, recording or otherwise, without the prior permission of the publisher.

The views and opinions expressed in this book are the author's own and the facts are as reported by her which have been verified to the extent possible, and the publishers are not in any way liable for the same.

ISBN: 978-93-5520-023-5

First impression 2021

10 9 8 7 6 5 4 3 2 1

The moral right of the author has been asserted.

Printed at Rakmo Press Pvt. Ltd, New Delhi

This book is sold subject to the condition that it shall not, by way of trade or otherwise, be lent, resold, hired out, or otherwise circulated, without the publisher's prior consent, in any form of binding or cover other than that in which it is published.

Dedicated to
Amma and Anna

Contents

The Makings of a Rishi / ix

1. Vasishtha / 1
2. Kasyapa / 25
3. Jamadagni / 48
4. Visvamitra / 75
5. Atri / 104
6. Bharadvaja / 129
7. Gotama / 164
8. The Seven Sages / 185

Acknowledgements / 199

Introduction

The Makings of a Rishi

The Vedas are known to be *apaurusheya* (not of human creation). They were revealed by Lord Brahma to certain persons who had attained spiritual knowledge by practising severe austerities. Thus, these persons came to be known as rishis. Since Vedic mantras were revealed to them, they were called *mantradrashtaarah* (seers of Vedic hymns). Bhrigu, Kavya, Prachetasa, Gritsamada, Nabha, Angirasa, Bharadvaja, Gargya, Kanva, Vamadeva, Kakshivanta, Kasyapa, Vatsara, Raibhya, Atri, Valgutaka, Vasishtha and Kundina were such rishis.

In the Rigveda, each *mandala* (book) is known to have been revealed to a particular rishi or his family. These mandalas are known as 'family books'. The rishi of the second mandala was Gritsamada; of the third mandala, Visvamitra; of the fourth, Vamadeva. Similarly, Atri, Bharadvaja, Vasishtha and Kanva are the seers of the fifth, sixth, seventh and eighth mandalas, respectively. The mantras of the first, ninth and tenth mandalas were contributed by various rishis. Sometimes, these rishis are also known as *mantrakritah* (composers of mantras) and *mantrapatayah* (masters of mantras) as the revealed mantras were later transmitted by them to their students who learned through *sravana* (hearing).

A person is not born a rishi; a person has to attain the status of a 'rishi'. He generally belonged to the *brahmavarna* (people of knowledge) as they were known in those days and obtained the status of rishi by *tapas* (austerity). The word 'rishi' means a person who is continuously on the move to know *rta*, the ultimate truth. The knowledge obtained in this process is utilized by them for the well-being and happiness of humanity at large. All branches of learning owe their allegiance to these great souls. The Vishnu Purana declares a rishi as one who knows *Parabrahman* (Supreme Spirit) abiding in the cavity of one's own heart. Such a person attains all his desires while being in Parabrahman.

A rishi is a person who has overcome *asuric* (demonic) qualities like anger, lust, greed, jealousy, arrogance, pride, ignorance and selfishness and has developed *daivii* (divine) attributes described in the Bhagavad Gita Verse 16.1–3. Some of the daivii qualities are purity of mind, charity, self-control, study of scriptures, austerity, uprightness, non-violence, truth, renunciation and forgiveness. A good definition of a rishi is available in the verse:

> *uurdhvaretah tapasyograh niyataasii ca samyamii*
> *saapaanugrahayoh saktah satyasandho bhaved rishih*

> A person who is chaste, stays in severe penance, controls his desire and the sense organs, who is a speaker of truth and has power to reward or punish is called a rishi.

Rishis may be rishis, *maharshis* and *brahmarshis*. A rishi could become a maharshi and then a brahmarshi through his *sadhana* (effort). Persons from the *kshatravarna* (political power wielding group) could only achieve the stature of a *rajarshi* through their tapas (for example, Janaka, Ikshvaku, Ambareesha, Sibi and Mandhata). Only one person, Visvamitra, though belonging to kshatravarna, is known to have attained the status of a brahmarshi after successively reaching the statuses of rishi, rajarshi and then maharshi, by performing severe tapas for long periods in all four quarters of the world. He was not satisfied when Lord Brahma himself conferred this status on him. He was happy only when he was accepted and endorsed by the greatest of sages—Sage Vasishtha. There is also a small class of *devarshis* (divine sages), for example, Narada and Parvata. Devarshis have the power to move around in all three worlds at their will.

Those who attain the highest level of knowledge of the Parabrahman are called brahmarshis, of whom the most well-known are Vasishtha, Visvamitra, Suka and the Sanat Kumaras. After the brahmarshis are the maharshis such as Sukracharya, Brihaspati, Kardama, Utathya, Vamadeva, Vishravas, Sakti and

Valakhilyas, who are revered for the *jnaana* (knowledge) they amassed.

Sages like Bharadvaja, Vajasravas, Parasara, Dadhici, Naciketa, Astavakra and Rishyasringa were *rishiputras* (sons of rishis), but became rishis by their own merit. Bhrigu, Marici, Atri, Angirasa, Pulaha, Kratu, Manu, Daksha, Vasishtha and Pulastya were the *maanasaputras* (born of the mind) of Lord Brahma. The maanasaputras were endowed by birth with the knowledge of the Parabrahman.

Only men need not be rishis. There are as many as 27 rishis mentioned in the Rigveda who were women. They are called *rishikaas*. Some of the well-known rishikaas are Ghoshaa, Godhaa, Visvavaara and Apala.

Rishis are known to be *satyavacasah* (speakers of truth). By the power of their tapas, they are capable of *anugraha* (reward) when pleased with a person's behaviour and service—for example, Sage Durvasa bestowed boons on Kunti for begetting sons from Devas. They are also prone to losing their temper when ignored or slighted, and for uttering *saapa* (curse). However, their anger dissipates quickly by appeasement and penitence and they will suggest the time and method of redemption from the curse. For example, Sage Durvasa cursed Sakuntala that she would be forgotten by her husband. After being entreated by her friends, he revealed how and when the curse would be lifted.

We human beings are advised to think twice before uttering something. We first form an idea in our mind and then choose the appropriate words to express that idea. However, rishis utter what they want to and it will be followed by the thought they mean to express.

There is a mantra in the Mahanarayana Upanishad Verse 12.4 in which individual instances of certain classes of beings are mentioned as *vibhutis* (personifications) of the Supreme Spirit: 'Lord Brahma among the Gods, the master of eloquence among the composers, the seer among the righteous people'. In the Bhagavad Gita, Krishna tells his disciple Arjuna some of his prominent vibhutis illustrative of his glory (for example, of the great sages, I am Bhrigu [10.25]; of the divine seers, I am Narada [10.26]; of the sages, I am Vyasa [10.37]).

The rishis are believed to reside in different quarters of the world to keep it in balance and harmony. Accordingly, Kausika, Yavakrita, Gargya, Galava and Kanva live in the eastern region; Svastyatreya, Namuchi, Pramuchi, Agastya, Sumukha and Vimukha live in the southern quarter; Nrshangu, Kavasha, Dhaumya and Kausheya live in the west and Vasishtha, Kasyapa, Atri, Visvamitra, Gotama, Jamadagni and Bharadvaja reside in the northern quarter. The last group of sages is known as saptarshis (seven sages).

A *manvantara*, in Hindu cosmology, is a cyclic period of time identifying the duration, reign or age of a Manu, the progenitor of mankind. There are 14 manvantaras of which we are now in the seventh ruled by Vaivasvata Manu. In each manvantara distinguished by the Manu who rules over it, seven rishis, certain deities, an Indra, a Manu and kings (sons of Manu) are created and perish. Vasishtha, Kasyapa, Jamadagni, Visvamitra, Atri, Bharadvaja and Gotama are the seven sages of the present *Vaivasvata Manvantara*. The seven sages are different in each cycle of four yugas (Krita, Treta, Dvapara and Kali). In contemporary western language, they correspond to the main stars in the Great Bear constellation.

The *Brihadaranyaka Upanishad* Verse 2.2.4 metaphorically describes the *indriyas* (the sense organs) as the seven rishis. The right and left ears are Gotama and Bharadvaja, respectively; the right and left eyes are Visvamitra and Jamadagni, respectively; the right and left nostrils are Vasishtha and Kasyapa, respectively, and *vaak* (tongue) is Atri, for through the tongue food is eaten. The saptarshis assist Siva, the *Adi Yogi* (first ascetic), to maintain the earth in a state of balance. Due to their spiritual and yogic powers, they have very long lifespans and are almost immortal. In fact, one can say that the saptarshis are not influenced by *samsara* (the cycle of life and death). They can see the future and are greater than Devas in power and piety.

It is said the seven sages once went to the Himalayas to meet Siva, but since he was engrossed in meditation, they had to wait for him to open his eyes. Siva, in order to test them, did not open his eyes for a long time. The sages did not display any emotion and continued to wait without any haste. Finally, after many years, Siva was pleased with the sages and opening his eyes, asked them to express their reason for seeking him. The sages asked Siva to explain the secret of his tranquillity. Siva blessed them with the secret knowledge of yoga and meditation. Thus, Siva became known as *Adi Guru* (first preceptor).

To conclude this section, we may cite a verse from *Uttararamacarita*, a drama by Bhavabhuti, in which the essential characteristics of a rishi are brought out beautifully in the following *sloka* (verse):

priyapraayaa vrittir vinayamadhuro vaaci niyamah
prakrityaa kalyaanii matir anavagiitah paricayah |
puro vaa pascaad vaa tadidam aviparyaasitarasam
rahasyam saadhuunaam anupadhi visuddham vijayate ||

Universal love and affection, extreme sweetness in speech, utter humility, genuine concern for the common good, an elegant dignity in demeanour: these are not adopted virtues but spring naturally from within and last forever as the greatest wealth of the rishis.

RISHIS AND GOTRAS

In Hindu society, the term 'gotra' broadly refers to people who have descended from an unbroken male lineage from a common male ancestor. Panini in *Astaadhyaayi* defines gotra for grammatical purposes as '*apatyampautraprabhrtigotram*' (4.1.162), which means the word 'gotra' denotes the progeny of a sage beginning with the son's son. It is said that the present gotra system prevalent among the people of India resulted from the seven sages and from Agastya as the eighth sage. Therefore, they are called *gotra pravartakas* (gotra propounders) of various *vamsas* (lineages).

The lineages are identified by two main attributes—the

gotra and the *pravara* (sub-lineage). The gotra indicates the chief clan to which an individual belongs. It is the name of the ancestor of a person by whose name his family has been known for generations. A pravara is constituted by the sage or sages who lived in the remote past, who were most illustrious and who are generally the ancestors of the gotra sages (seven sages and Agastya). Both the gotra and pravara are identified with rishis who were part of the lineage. The gotra is always identified by the name of a single rishi (for example, Bharadvaja Gotra) while the pravara may have a number of rishis (up to seven) associated with it.

However, most of the pravaras consist of only three rishis. To illustrate, a person who belongs to Kasyapa Gotra—the clan of Sage Kasyapa—could further belong to a *tryaarsheyapravara* (a cluster consisting of the names of three rishis) of Kasyapa, Avatsara and Aasita. A person belonging to Bharadvaja Gotra could have a tryaarsheyapravara of Aangirasa, Baarhaspatya and Bhaaradvaja. In Jamadagni Gotra, a pravara could consist of five rishis: Bhaargava, Cyavana, Aapnavana, Aurva and Jaamadagnya. Lohita Gotra has only two rishis—Visvamitra and Devarata—as pravara.

Even today, in many traditional families, the custom of offering prostrations to an elder is by distinctly stating one's gotra and pravara. This is termed as *gotraabhivandana*. In daily worship, one mentions not only the name of the specific founder of one's gotra and the rishi who founded it but also the pravara.

1

Vasishtha

sivadhyaanaratam saantam tridasairapi puujitam |
*brahmasuunum mahaatmaanam vasishtham puujayet sadaa ||**

Vasishtha, Lord Brahma's son, is venerable and worshipped even by the gods. He is composed and always immersed in meditating on the Parabrahman.

VASISHTHA: FOREMOST AMONG RISHIS

The purpose of human life is the realization of the Self. In each yuga, the Parabrahman or the Absolute manifests as Lord Brahma, Vishnu and Siva (Trinity), who in turn

---

*Visvanatha, *Vratacuudaamani*, Vaavilla Ramaswamy Sastrulu and Sons, Chennai, 1935.

engage in *srishti* (creation), *sthiti* (maintenance) and *pralaya* (destruction) of the world. These three are called personal gods and are one level lower than the Parabrahman.

When Lord Brahma desired to bring forth the world, he first created from his mind the four Kumaras: Sanatkumara, Sanaka, Sanandana and Sanatana. However, to Lord Brahma's great dismay, they were determined to remain celibate and undertook the *nivrittimaarga* or the path of renunciation. Lord Brahma then created the *prajapatis* (leaders of all creatures) and directed them to undertake the *pravrittimaarga* or path of action. Both paths are enunciated in the Vedas and both are necessary for the harmony of this world. Sage Vasishtha is the most important of all sages, who took to the path of action not only for his own good but for the good of the world.

Vasishtha is the foremost of the saptarshis and he attained this position by dint of his severe austerity and control over senses. He is Lord Brahma's maanasaputra and was known for doing *japa* (repeating prayers in a murmur) constantly. He not only attained siddhi, the highest level of knowledge, in the mastery of the Vedas but also attained fame as the seer of the seventh mandala of the Rigveda. Vasishtha was one of the nine prajapatis and a hymn in the Rigveda is dedicated to him. He married Arundhati, the daughter of Kardama and Devahuti, and settled down with her in a hermitage on the banks of the Sarasvati River. His wife was an epitome of devotion and virtue. She was a perfect match for Vasishtha's erudition. To this day, newly-wed couples are directed to seek the blessings of Vasishtha and Arundhati as part of the wedding rituals. The couple is shown the star representing sage Vasishtha and a small star close to it as Arundhati.

VASISHTHA: KULAGURU OF IKSHVAKU DYNASTY

In the Tretayuga, Vasishtha became the kulaguru (priest of the dynasty) of the Ikshvaku race. The Ikshvaku race or the Solar dynasty began with Vivasvan or Surya, the Sun God, who begot Manu and he, in turn, begot Ikshvaku. Vasishtha, with his immense knowledge and scholarship, was the guiding light for the Ikshvaku kings: from Dilipa to Raghu to Aja to Dasaratha to Lord Rama.

Initially, when requested, Sage Vasishtha had declined to accept the position of kulaguru as he did not wish to get involved in worldly affairs. However, his father Lord Brahma hinted that Lord Narayana himself would be born as Sri Rama in the Ikshvaku Dynasty and Vasishtha would get the privilege to become Sri Rama's preceptor. Sage Vasishtha then accepted the post of kulaguru and taught Sri Rama the much-needed lessons in kingship and statecraft and the use of all kinds of weapons, as well as preached to him *brahmatattva*, the ultimate truth. During his early years, Sage Vasishtha ably guided the kings of the Ikshvaku race, but after his fallout with King Nimi (discussed later in this chapter), he decided to remain as the priest of only the descendants of King Raghu, that is, Raghuvamsa—the lineage in which Sri Rama was prophesied to be born.

Sage Vasishtha had dug a well in his asrama and with his powers, made it a source of the Sarayu River. Once due to drought in Ayodhya, the people suffered from thirst and hunger. The then ruler, King Ikshvaku, came to Sage Vasishtha and pleaded for his people's well-being. The magnanimous Vasishtha prayed to the Sarayu, requesting her to flow towards Ayodhya and eliminate the grief of the land. From that day, the Sarayu came to be known as Aikshvaaki and Vaasishthi.

When King Dilipa and his wife Sudakshina remained childless for several years, they approached Sage Vasishtha for his blessings to have children. Sage Vasishtha advised the couple to serve the celestial Nandini who was the calf of the wish-fulfilling cow Kaamadhenu. She had round patches all over her body and hence she was also called Shabalaa (multicoloured). Nandini, like her mother, was capable of satisfying any and every need of her master. Vasishtha looked upon Nandini as his own daughter.

Noticing the look of surprise on King Dilipa's face, Vasishtha explained: 'King Dilipa, do you not remember the time when you were returning from Indra's palace after having helped him vanquish demons? You were in a haste to return to your kingdom and meet your wife, who was entering your chambers after her monthly separation from you. I am aware that according to the Sastras, the king has to be present when the queen returns from her menstruation. Unfortunately, in your haste, you didn't show your respect to the celestial cow Kaamadhenu who cursed you in anger to remain childless.'

With his powers, Vasishtha had been able to see into King Dilipa's past where he had failed to pay obeisance to the divine Kaamadhenu, who was resting under the Kalpavriksha (celestial wish-fulfilling tree). The queen blushed and bowed her head while the King's face showed remorse. Sage Vasishtha continued, 'I advise you both to serve and please Nandini, the daughter of Kaamadhenu, and seek her blessings to obtain progeny.'

Accordingly, King Dilipa and his wife Sudakshina began to serve Nandini in all earnestness and humility. They would escort her to graze, clean the cowshed, milk her and make beds of hay for her to rest at night. In this manner, they served Nandini for 21 days without rest or respite.

One day, a lion attacked Nandini and to save her, King Dilipa offered himself as food to the lion. Nandini was immensely pleased with the king's actions and she addressed him in a human voice. 'O King, the appearance of the lion was only an illusion created by me to test you. I am immensely pleased with the love and affectionate service that you and your wife have rendered unto me. You will be blessed with a son who will make you proud. May your dynasty flourish.' She bade King Dilipa and Sudakshina return to their kingdom. Soon after, the king and queen became proud parents of a baby boy. In this manner, Sage Vasishtha guided King Dilipa and Sudakshina in discharging their royal duties.

Similarly, King Dasaratha who was childless for a long time sought the blessings and advice of Sage Vasishtha: 'I have advanced in years and deteriorated in strength. No more am I the Dasaratha who fought alongside Indra against the demons and vanquished them. Now, I am Dasaratha, a doddering old man. I married several times to avoid death by the axe of the wrathful Parashurama, but none of my wives were able to give me a son. Who will perform my last rites? Whom shall I name as my successor? Who will take care of my kingdom and my people, who are verily like my own children?'

It was under the guidance of Vasishtha that Sage Rishyasringa was brought from Angadesa to perform the *putrakameshti yajna* (a sacrifice to beget a son) for Dasaratha. Once the *yajna* (a sacrifice to the gods) was completed, a divine person came out of the sacrificial fire and handed over a vessel containing payasam to King Dasaratha. The person spoke thus, 'O King, the gods are pleased with your prayers and wish to grant you a boon. You will be blessed with male children. Please distribute this payasam among your wives. They will, in due course of time, be blessed with children.'

King Dasaratha divided the payasam into two parts and gave one part to Kausalya, his eldest wife. Out of the other half in his hand, he gave half to Sumitra. Of the remaining one-fourth, he gave half to Kaikeyi. He gave the remaining portion to Sumitra again. Thus, Rama, Lakshmana, Bharata and Satrughna were born.

Rama was the eldest son and was born to Kausalya, Bharata was born to Kaikeyi. Since Sumitra received two portions, she gave birth to two sons, the twins Lakshmana and Satrughna. It is said that Lakshmana was born from the portion of payasam given to Sumitra first time and, therefore, was devoted to Rama, while Satrughna followed Bharata as he was born from the second portion given to her again at the end. In fact, it was at Vasishtha's behest that the sons born to Dasaratha were named Rama, Lakshmana, Bharata and Satrughna.

As the four children were growing up, Sage Vasishtha taught them various arts and skills. He was their guide, mentor and philosopher. Once, Sage Visvamitra approached Dasaratha and asked him to let Rama and Lakshmana accompany him to end the demonic activities of the rakshasas (demons) Subaahu and Maarica ahead of a yajna Visvamitra wished to perform. Dasaratha was most reluctant and it was Sage Vasishtha who convinced him that it was imperative to accede to Sage Visvamitra's request. By following Vasishtha's advice and sending his sons with Visvamitra, Dasaratha also protected his people from the wrath of Sage Visvamitra, who would have cursed everyone had he been refused the help he had requested.

As the kulaguru of King Dasaratha, Vasishtha was Sri Rama's first tutor. Besides teaching the first lessons of *kshatravidyaa* (the arts of archery and warfare), Vasishtha imparted the highest knowledge of the Self to Sri Rama. The spiritual knowledge imparted by Sage Vasishtha to Sri Rama forms the central message of the Yoga Vaasishtha. Through replies to questions posed by Sri Rama, Sage Vasishtha explained the many wonders of the cosmos, the wheel of samsara and the need for realization of Self. Vasishtha was also the author of Vaasishtha Samhitaa and some parts of

Agnipurana and Vishnupurana. Along with other saptarshis, he composed Saptarshi Ramayana, with each rishi being responsible for composing one verse narrating the events of one of the *kaandas* (sections) of the Valmiki Ramayana.

VASISHTHA AND ARUNDHATI

Kardamaprajapati was one of the nine sons of Lord Brahma. He was a maanasaputra, a great yogi and a sage. He lived on the banks of Sarasvati River and taught the sacred lore to his disciples, as was the practice in those days. He performed severe penance and pleased Lord Vishnu, who granted him two boons—first, a worthy wife and second, to have Lord Vishnu himself be born as his son. After receiving these two boons, Kardama decided to become a recluse; he devoted his remaining life to Lord Vishnu once the boons were fulfilled.

Kardama married Devahuti, the daughter of King Manu and his wife Satarupa. She bore him nine daughters and one son. Arundhati was one of their daughters. Sage Atri's wife Anasuya was Arundhati's sister. Kapila, who taught his mother about the Parabrahman, was their brother. From her childhood, Arundhati was more interested in listening to her father and learning the sacred lore than in other duties of the hermitage or in playing with her friends. Many a time she would forget even to milk the cows, which was her duty, lost in listening to her father teaching his students. In consonance with her character, Kardama arranged her marriage with Sage Vasishtha, who was known to be a very learned man.

After her marriage, Arundhati went to live with her husband, and there too she would finish her household chores well in time to join her husband's classes. She soon learned and understood the essence of the Vedas and the Puranas.

One day, after Sage Vasishtha had explained the need for purity in thought and action to his disciples, his eyes fell upon his wife, who was listening with rapt attention. He asked her if she had understood. Arundhati seized the opportunity and entreated him to allow her to continue teaching the lesson to the class. Vasishtha acquiesced and was greatly surprised by her clarity of thought and perfect enunciation. He said, 'Arundhati! I am impressed by your knowledge and expression. I am blessed to have you as my wife. From today, I would like you to help me in the class as well.'

Arundhati bore Vasishtha a 100 sons, of whom Sakti was the eldest. Parasara, Sakti's son, authored *Parasarasmriti*, a canonical law book. His son—Vasishtha's great-grandson—Vedavyasa, arranged the four Vedas and authored the Mahabharata, the Harivamsa and the 18 Puranas.

Lord Brahma had gifted Nandini, Kaamadhenu's calf, to Vasishtha and Arundhati, so that they could perform their austerities with ease. She bestowed immense quantities of milk for the preparation of ghee, butter and other products required to perform yajnas and other sacrificial rites. As Nandini, like her mother, was a wish-fulfilling cow, she could grant anything that Vasishtha desired as long as he wanted it for the good and welfare of the world. Indeed, it was with her blessings that Vasishtha and Arundhati led a very meritorious life. One day, the eight Vasus (deities and Indra's attendants) and their wives came to Vasishtha's hermitage after spending the day in the groves nearby. Sage Vasishtha, as was his practice, welcomed the Vasus and their spouses and served them with food and drink. Seeing the rich and lavish spread, the Vasus enquired the source, and Sage Vasishtha told them all about the cow Nandini and her divine powers. Arundhati, who was observing the changing expressions of the Vasus, intervened. 'My husband has not mentioned that Nandini is the reason for his long-standing rivalry with Sage Visvamitra.'

Yet when the Vasus saw the holy cow, they became overwhelmed with greed and paying no heed to Arundhati's words, carried it away. The Vasus justified their action by insisting that the cow would be more useful to them than to Sage Vasishtha. The next day, when Vasishtha realized that Nandini was missing, he divined what had occurred. He cursed the Vasus to be born on earth as mortals. By then, the Vasus had understood the enormity of their action and, returning to Vasishtha's hermitage with Nandini, they pleaded with him for forgiveness. However, Vasishtha was in no mood to forgive them. The Vasus and their wives fell at the feet of Arundhati and begged for mercy. They appealed to the mother in her to reveal a path for their release from the curse, as they were aware that a curse once uttered cannot be undone. They held her feet and begged forgiveness till she relented.

She approached her husband and requested Vasishtha to

forgive them. 'You know that I cannot withdraw my curse but I shall modify it for your sake. The first seven Vasus would return to the heavens immediately after birth. Only the eighth Vasu, who was the main culprit, will have to suffer a full life on earth. Let them approach Gangaa to be their mother.' The Vasus were, therefore, born to King Santanu and the divine Gangaa in the Mahabharata.

After this incident, Arundhati felt that it would be for the best to allow Nandini to return to the heavens. Nandini had attracted attention from the Vasus and King Visvaratha, who later became Sage Visvamitra through his tapas. Both had desired the wealth that she was capable of giving and had tried to attain her by force against the wishes of Sage Vasishtha. In the case of Visvaratha, Sage Vasishtha had been able to protect Nandini from him. However, the Vasus had managed to lead her away. Nandini had not taken any action to save herself as Sage Vasishtha was asleep at that time. Although Sage Vasishtha knew this would hamper his austerities, he followed Arundhati's advice.

Once Nandini left Vasishtha's abode, the days of plenitude were no more. Vasishtha and Arundhati faced difficult times. Their gurukula (school) was also temporarily closed. Sage Vasishtha decided to go with other sages to the Himalayas for penance. He told Arundhati to stay back and take care of the hermitage in his absence and left.

After several months of austerities in the Himalayas, the sages wanted to return to their homes but landslides and heavy snowfall prevented their return. In Sage Vasishtha's absence, there was famine and Arundhati had to subsist on roots. Sage Vasishtha prayed to Lord Siva for Arundhati's well-being, while Arundhati prayed to God for the same for her husband.

One day, a boy came to the hermitage and begged for some food. Arundhati had nothing to offer and could only give him some roasted seeds. After eating the seeds, the boy asked if he could join Sage Vasishtha's gurukula. Arundhati immediately told him about Sage Vasishtha's absence and suggested that she be his teacher until her husband returned. The boy agreed and stayed on. He began to help Arundhati around the hermitage and also took lessons from her.

On his return, Sage Vasishtha was pleasantly surprised to see that Arundhati was hale and healthy and also that there was a student for him to teach. Arundhati told him that the boy had taken care of her in the difficult time of famine. Sage Vasishtha turned to thank the boy and his joy knew no bounds when it was Lord Siva who stood before him, magnificent in his splendour and glory. Goddess Parvati accompanied him. They blessed Sage Vasishtha and Arundhati and said, 'Both of you prayed for the other's safety. We are touched by your devotion to each other. We bless that you be happy together and act as an example to mankind regarding the sanctity of married life.' After the divine couple disappeared, Sage Vasishtha embraced his wife as she fell at his feet and they lived many more years spending time in prayer and austerities.

VASISHTHA AND VISVAMITRA

Vasishtha performed several sacrifices, practised austerities and made offerings to the gods as was wont of seekers of truth. The Vedas declare that humans and gods are joined in a symbiotic relationship. Men perform yajnas and yagas to propitiate Devas and they, in turn, bless the humans with abundance of rain, cattle, foodgrains, etc.

Sage Vasishtha and Arundhati never desired worldly wealth or riches and led an austere life. Guests were always welcome at their hermitage and they were treated with respect and love. The couple rigorously followed the Hindu custom of treating the guest as god.

Once, King Visvaratha came to his hermitage and Vasishtha honoured him and his large army with a magnificent feast befitting the royal entourage. Visvaratha became eager to know the secret of Vasishtha's wealth. Initially, Vasishtha evaded the king's questions and did not reveal anything about Nandini, but King Visvaratha persisted. When he came to know about the wish-fulfilling nature of Nandini, he made an offer to trade her for land and riches.

But Vasishtha wanted nothing as Nandini fulfilled his every need. King Visvaratha spoke haughtily, threatening Sage Vasishtha with dire consequences. Visvaratha tried to seize Nandini by force but was unsuccessful. This failure to exercise his might as well as Vasishtha's subsequent forgiveness was a blow to his pride. It spurred Visvaratha to give up his kingdom in exchange for a long and strenuous life of austerity to attain the status of a brahmarshi like Vasishtha. All of Visvaratha's power was swallowed by Vasishtha's *brahmadanda* (staff imbued with the power of Parabrahman). The brahmadanda represents the Parabrahman; all things get absorbed into it. All things are composed of *gunas* (*sattva, rajas and tamas*) and are absorbed into *nirguna* (Parabrahman) just as the seven colours combine to become white light. Visvaratha left Vasishtha's hermitage ashamed, but continued his austerities and attacked Vasishtha repeatedly. Their confrontations continued for ages before realization dawned on Visvaratha and their enmity ended.

Another instance of their rivalry revolves around King Hariscandra of the Ikshvaku race. Vasishtha was the preceptor of King Hariscandra too. King Hariscandra always abided by the truth and was famous for his *satyavaadi* (always uttering the truth) nature. Once, in the court of Indra amidst all, Vasishtha had declared that King Hariscandra would stand by the truth under all circumstances—he was the embodiment of truth. Hearing this, Visvaratha challenged him and swore to prove Vasishtha wrong. At this point, Visvaratha still considered Vasishtha as his enemy. He scornfully declared, 'The embodiment of truth? I cannot accept your word. Do I not know the nature of men? When circumstances turn unfavourable, even the most truthful and righteous person will bend. I, Visvaratha, will prove to all in this assembly how wrong you are.'

Visvaratha set many trials and tribulations for King Hariscandra but the king did not swerve from the path of truth. Finally, Visvaratha had to concede defeat and admit that Vasishtha was right.

VASISHTHA CURSES SAUDASA

Mitrasaha, son of Sudasa, king of the Ikshvaku race, was married to Madayanti. Once, when Mitrasaha, or Saudasa as he was more popularly known, went to the forest to hunt, he killed a demon. The demon's brother, when attacked by Saudasa, sought his mercy. At his plea, Saudasa let him go and returned to his kingdom. The demon's brother, however, decided to avenge his brother's death and followed King Saudasa to his palace. He changed his guise, became a cook in the palace and waited for an opportune time.

Once, when Sage Vasishtha arrived at the royal palace, the King received him cordially and invited Sage Vasishtha to join him for lunch. When they were seated, the demon cook served Sage Vasishtha human flesh. Vasishtha stood up, his face aflame in fury. He took a few drops of water from his *kamandalu* (water-pot), uttered an incantation and sprinkled the water on the king. The sage cursed King Mitrasaha to become a demon.

When Saudasa felt the drops of water on his body and heard the curse, he was shocked. He could not believe that his kulaguru, whom he worshipped, had cursed him! How could Sage Vasishtha attribute such an action to him? He lost control of his senses and, in turn, took water in his palm.

Madayanti, who was watching in horror, approached him

in one swift movement and held his hand. When Mitrasaha turned his face towards her, she shook her head. 'No, my Lord! What are you doing? Sage Vasishtha is our kulaguru.' Mitrasaha felt ashamed and sprinkled the water on his own feet. At once, his feet became spotted with black marks and, having changed into a demon, he left the palace. He became known as Kalmashapada (one with spotted feet) and roamed the forests devouring people and destroying homes.

When Sage Vasishtha narrated the incident to his wife, Arundhati's response was, 'My Lord, King Saudasa has always behaved with utmost propriety towards us. I would like to believe he was unaware of the matter, please do not be hasty in judging him.' With his mystic powers, Vasishtha realized that the cook-demon had served him flesh without King Saudasa's knowledge. Vasishtha was overcome with remorse. He told his wife, 'What have I done! In my haste and anger, I cursed Saudasa to become a demon. I must atone for my error of judgement; I will perform 12 years of penance to purify myself.'

Wandering in the forest, Kalmashapada chanced upon a couple enjoying conjugal bliss. Under the influence of demonic tendencies, he pounced on the man and devoured him despite the wife's pleading. The wife, therefore, cursed the King, 'Just as you have wrought this sorrow unto me, so shall you die if you consort with your wife.' Saudasa continued on his way without heeding her words, as in his demonic form, he had no awareness of his sins.

Vasishtha, on his return from penance, found that Saudasa had been released from his demonic state by Sage Uttanka.

However, Saudasa, who craved for progeny, could not couple with his wife because of the curse. King Saudasa and Madayanti begged Sage Vasishtha for an offspring so that the royal line could continue. Vasishtha blessed the couple and Madayanti became pregnant. However, she could not deliver the child. Moved by pity, Vasishtha struck her abdomen with a stone and a son was born, who was therefore named Asmaka (crushed by a stone).

VASISHTHA: GREAT-GRANDFATHER OF VEDAVYASA

One day, Kalmashapada came across Sakti, the eldest son of Sage Vasishtha. Unable to recognize him, the king-demon pounced on him, killing him in one stroke. Kalmashapada did not stop with this, he entered Vasishtha's hermitage and killed all his other sons too. Only Arundhati and Sakti's pregnant wife, Adrushyanti, who had gone to the nearby river, survived.

When Vasishtha saw the bodies of his dear sons, he could not control his grief. Without uttering a word to his wife or daughter-in-law, he tied himself with ropes and jumped into the Sarasvati. The river, however, split into a thousand streams and prevented his death. Vasishtha came ashore and saw Sakti's wife Adrushyanti waiting for him and seeking his protection. From her womb came the sound of the chanting of the Vedas. Vasishtha took courage and escorted her to the hermitage, where Arundhati was awaiting their return. He could not face Arundhati's accusatory look. 'If you, who are well-versed in scriptures, attempt suicide, then what of lesser mortals? The scriptures unequivocally declare that dying by suicide is akin to condemning yourself to eternal damnation. It also does not behove you to run away from your responsibilities,' she told him. After some months, Adrushyanti gave birth to a son and Vasishtha named him Parasara.

When Parasara grew up and learned about his father's death, he wanted to perform a yajna and kill all demons. Vasishtha advised him to take the path of patience and forgiveness. Vasishtha told Parasara not to waste his religious merit and instead work for the welfare of mankind.

Later, Parasara begot Vedavyasa, who had a son, Suka, who had realized Parabrahman. When the son of Abhimanyu and grandson of Arjuna, Parikshit, the ruler of Hastinapur after Yudhishthira, realized that he would be dying in a week's time, it was Suka who recited the Bhagavata Purana for him to attain salvation. Thus, Vasishtha sired an illustrious lineage.

VASISHTHA AND NIMI

Manu, the forerunner of Tretayuga, fathered Ikshvaku, who was the progenitor of the illustrious Ikshvaku race to which Sri Rama belonged. This is the story of Vasishtha and King Ikshvaku's twelfth son, Nimi, who eventually became the founder of the Videha Kingdom and the ancestor of King Janaka, the father of Sita.

King Nimi was valorous and expanded his kingdom through victorious wars, whereby the kingdom came to be known as Vaijayanta. He was a great king and ruled over his people justly and wisely. His kingdom resembled a heavenly abode in peace and prosperity, and he was loved by one and all.

As stated previously, Sage Vasishtha was the kulaguru of the Ikshvaku race, and was held in high esteem by King Nimi. The latter decided to perform a special sacrifice, which would take many years to complete, thinking that it would delight his father and bring prosperity to his subjects. He wanted to approach Sage Vasishtha, the foremost among the brahmarshis, to be the *hotar* (main priest) at the ritual. He also decided to invite three other maanasaputras—Atri, Angirasa and Bhrigu—to serve as *ritviks* (other officiating priests).

Nimi addressed Vasishtha thus, 'O Great Sage! You have been the benefactor of our royal lineage and guided us through several difficult times. I am now interested in performing austerities for the good of all. Please accept the mantle of chief preceptor for conducting the event.'

Sage Vasishtha was taken by surprise at this request and said, 'O King, I am honoured to be invited. But I must tell you that this great ritual takes several years to complete. I have already been invited to a similar yajna by the king of Devas, Indra. His yajna will also last several years. Since I have already given him my word, I must hasten there. I know you will understand and wait for my return to perform the sacrifice you have in mind.' The king was so taken aback that he could not find words to answer.

Taking Nimi's silence to mean that he would wait for his return, Vasishtha left for Indra's abode. Nimi returned to his palace plagued with thoughts: '*I need to think of the welfare of my people. That is my prime duty. It will be a long wait for the sage's return...What happens if bad times befall the kingdom in the meantime? I did not agree openly to Sage Vasishtha's suggestion, so why waste these years in waiting? I am sure Sage Vasishtha will understand my anxiety and accept my decision to start the yajna without him. Surely, my duty towards my people explains my decision.'* And so it was that King Nimi decided to go ahead and perform the yajna with the help of other sages. He invited Sage Gotama to be the hotar and, having obtained his assent, started the yajna.

Sage Vasishtha spent almost 5,000 years with Lord Indra, helping him complete the yajna. Once it was over, Indra implored him to stay back for some more time. But he said, 'I must hurry back now as King Nimi has been waiting for me all this while,' and returned forthwith to Nimi's kingdom. To his shock, he learned that the king had not chosen to wait and the great yajna was being performed without him. Vasishtha was furious with Nimi and rushed to his palace to confront him. But as it was night by the time he reached, Nimi had retired for the day and did not receive him. This added fuel to the fire since he felt doubly insulted. Not only was he, the kulaguru, not received by the king, but it also appeared that Nimi had no intention of explaining what had happened! How dare Nimi slight the great sage? And in a burst of rage, Vasishtha thundered a terrible curse on the hapless king: 'It is your ego that made you break your word and go ahead. Therefore, may consciousness leave your body now!' And he stormed out of the palace towards his hermitage.

The effect of Sage Vasishtha's curse was immediate. Nimi's spirit left his sleeping body. But Nimi was no ordinary king, having attained a higher level of consciousness through meditation and good deeds. He became aware of what had happened and thought, *'Sage Vasishtha has cursed me but I was asleep and not informed about his arrival at the palace. I cannot be at fault… I had never agreed to wait for his return from Indra's service to begin the yajna. Why should he then curse me thus, despite not having wronged him? This is unjust! Therefore, I too shall curse him.'* Hence, Nimi's spirit cursed thus, 'O Sage Vasishtha! May you suffer the same way you have punished me. May you lose consciousness, and thereby lose the ability to perform austerities ordained by the sastras!'

Vasishtha had reached his hermitage when consciousness left his body and he fell down dead. His physical remains were cremated duly by his family. And so it was that the king and his preceptor became cursed at the same time. Both lost their physical bodies and remained in the form of ethereal spirit.

But Vasishtha was no ordinary soul. He went to his father, Lord Brahma, and with folded hands, pleaded, 'Please show me the way out. I acknowledge I was harsh on King Nimi and, therefore, by his curse, my body was taken away. But there must be some way for me to get a new body without having to undergo the usual cycle of birth and death. Help me, O Father!' Lord Brahma spent some time in contemplation and then advised Vasishtha's soul thus, 'Enter the semen of Varuna and you will find the way out of this.' Vasishtha did as advised and waited patiently inside Varuna for a new body.

One day, Varuna's eyes fell on the most beautiful celestial nymph, Urvasi, who was playing in Varuna's garden. Attracted by her voluptuous and youthful beauty, Varuna stepped before her and passionately expressed his great desire for her, making the maiden shiver with joy and surprise. Trembling and blushing, Urvasi responded thus, 'O Varuna, your passion sweeps me off my feet! How can any woman resist your charm! But I have already said yes to Mitra, who is waiting for me ahead on this path. Alas, it is my fate that I must go.' Urvasi sighed despondently and turned around to continue on her way, glancing back frequently at Varuna with yearning.

Varuna's desire rose with every movement she made and, unable to control himself, he let his seed into an earthen pot. Vasishtha had been awaiting release from Varuna's body, and this was his moment! From the pot rose a new body which was immediately occupied by Vasishtha's soul. Thus, Vasishtha got a new body which was *ayonija* (not born of a womb).

Meanwhile, in Nimi's kingdom, the great sage Bhrigu and many other priests continued the yajna. Nimi's embalmed body lay in bed, while they finished all the related rituals successfully. After the yajna was over, they prayed to the gods who had been propitiated by the yajna to give them a boon and resurrect their beloved King Nimi. The gods agreed and called for the soul of Nimi to appear before them.

Nimi's soul had, in the meantime, gained greater spiritual power as a result of him having immersed himself in meditation. He had realized the Self and had found ultimate bliss. Therefore, Nimi did not want to enter his mortal body and go through the cycle of birth and death again. But at the same time, he could not bear the sorrow of his people either. So he proposed thus to the gods who wanted him to take up his body: 'O great ones! I am greatly obliged to you for your offer. But in the time between losing my body and the completion of the yajna, several years have passed. I have achieved the highest level of self-realization and no longer wish to come back to earth in a mortal body. Yet I wish to remain with my beloved subjects. Please make it so that I may stay as the air on their eyelids.' The gods were deeply impressed by Nimi's love for his people and agreed to this strange request. And so that Nimi may have some rest, since he was now in the form of wind on the eyelids of people, the gods ensured that we blink, and the time taken to blink came to be known as *nimisha*. Since the gods do not blink, they are called *animishas*.

The subjects of King Nimi realized that though their king lived with them on their eyelids, the physical absence of a real king meant that they had no protector and no one to rule them. Soon, the kingdom would be beset by problems. So they approached the sages who had helped in the yajna for a remedy to the new crisis. Since King Nimi's body had been preserved, the sages decided to use it with great skill. Using the tremendous concentrated power of their minds and deep Vedic knowledge, they churned the physical remains of King Nimi with *arani*—a charmed branch of the Bombax tree—along with prayers and chants. In due course of time, this agitated mass was transformed, and in its place appeared a baby boy, glowing like the sun. The baby was named Mithi since he emerged out of *mathana* (churning). He grew up to establish a great lineage called Maithila. This clan is also known by his other name—Vaideha—since he was born from the body of his father. King Nimi, from whose body rose Mithi or Vaideha, was the ancestor of King Janaka, the father of Sita. Thus, the Ikshvaku dynasty, which branched into two after Nimi, was united with the marriage of Sri Rama and Sita.

And so it came to pass that both the sage and the king cursed each other and lived out their curses. But since both were great men, the curses did not have the power to completely destroy them. Instead, they led to new beginnings.

2

Kasyapa

kasyapah sarvalokaadhyah sarvasaastraarthakovidah |
aatmayogabalenaiva srishtisthityantakaarakah ||*

Kasyapa is the father of mankind, an expert in spiritual knowledge and is capable of creation, sustenance and dissolution by his own spiritual power.

KASYAPA: PROGENITOR OF ALL RACES

In every manvantara, Lord Brahma, the Creator, creates maanasaputras with his manas (mind). These maanasaputras take on the mantle of assisting Lord Brahma. In the beginning, only Marici, Atri, Angirasa, Pulastya, Pulaha, Kratu, Pracetasa,

---

*Visvanatha, *Vratacuudaamani*, Vaavilla Ramaswamy Sastrulu and Sons, Chennai, 1935.

Vasishtha, Bhrigu and Narada were the maanasaputras. Later, Kardama, Vikrita, Sesha, Samsraya, Bahuputra, Sthanu, Daksha, Vivasvan, Arishtanemi and Kasyapa joined the ranks. Of these that Lord Brahma created, Marici, Angirasa, Pulastya, Pulaha, Kratu and Pracetasa followed his instructions and became prajapatis, whereas Narada, Sanatkumara, Sanaka, Sanandana and Sanatana did not. The latter group chose not to get entangled in the snares of samsara and renounced the world. Sage Kasyapa was one of the prajapatis who followed Lord Brahma's directions and helped the Creator populate the world with various kinds of beings.

Kasyapa was born to Sage Marici and his wife Kalaa, the daughter of Kardama and Devahuti. He was the youngest of the prajapatis. Kasyapa means 'turtle' in Sanskrit. In the Vedas, the term 'Kasyapa' is explained as the reversed form of *pasyaka* (seer). Pasyaka is explained as the one who sees the reality.

Sage Kasyapa married several times, and with many of his wives sired entire races, separate and distinct from the others. Many of his wives were Dakshaprajapati's daughters. Daksha, born to Lord Brahma, married Prasuti, a daughter of Svayambhuva Manu and Satarupa. They had 60 daughters. Dakshaprajapati gave many of his daughters in marriage, 13 in total, to Sage Kasyapa: Aditi, Diti, Danu, Kaalaka, Taamra, Krodhavasa, Manu, Anala, Arishta, Vinata, Kadru, Puloma and Somathi. However, all 13 daughters were not given at the same time. Sage Kasyapa married them singly, in pairs and so on. He had several hermitages and his wives lived sometimes by themselves and sometimes in pairs. With some of his wives, Sage Kasyapa had brief relationships, possibly only for the purpose of fathering particular children. Aditi and Diti were married off first and lived with Sage Kasyapa for several years. Both served him with diligence and were blessed with numerous children. Like Aditi and Diti, Kadru and Vinata were given away together to Sage Kasyapa. However, the relationship between Kadru and Vinata soured, and Vinata had to suffer a lot at the hands of Kadru.

Kasyapa, Aditi and Diti

Aditi and Diti were the first of Dakshaprajapati's daughters to be married to Sage Kasyapa. Aditi bore him 33 children, who came to be known as Devas, further divided into groups of 12 Adityas, 11 Rudras, eight Vasus and the Ashvini twins. She first birthed Dhata and Aryama; then Mitra and Varuna; then Amsa and Bhaga and lastly, Indra and Vivasvan. The remaining four Adityas (Vishnu, Tvashta, Pushan and Savitar) were born to her later. The eight Vasus include Dhara, Dhruva, Soma, Aha, Anala, Anila, Prabhasa and Pratyusha, and the Rudras comprise Ajaikapat, Ahirbudhnya, Pinaki, Aparajita, Rta, Pitrirupa, Tryambaka, Vrshakapi, Sambhu, Havana and Isvara. Aditi was also chosen by Lord Vishnu as his mother when he took his fifth incarnation as Vamana. All of her children grew up to be of fine character and became gods after drinking amrita (the nectar of immortality). Vivasvan started the Suryavansha (Solar dynasty) and his grandson Ikshvaku renamed his pedigree as the Ikshvakus, which later became famous as the lineage in which Sri Rama, son of Dasaratha, was born.

Diti, who was a silent spectator to the birth of Aditi's children, was consumed by jealousy. One evening, Sage Kasyapa was completing his evening rituals. Aditi was away from the hermitage. Diti felt that the time was appropriate to approach her husband. She ignored the injunction that at the time of sunset, one must not indulge in certain acts. She applied sandal paste and adornments before approaching her husband.

Kasyapa, seeing the desire in her eyes, was irritated at being disturbed when he was performing his spiritual duties. He looked at Diti and, keeping his annoyance in check, explained to her, 'Dearest Diti, I am engaged in the spiritual rites that will bring welfare to us all. You have helped me so far but now you seem to have forgotten yourself. Don't you see that it is already dusk? This is an inauspicious time and is ruled by Rudra with his *ganas* (followers). Please leave now.' Diti advanced, and seating herself beside him, placed her palm on his thigh. Kasyapa tried again, 'Diti, the result of your inappropriate behaviour will hurt you forever. Pray heed my words.' And he moved her hand away from him. Diti was in no state to listen. She was besotted and said, 'My love! I am but a part of you and need you to complete me now.' She indicated that Kasyapa should honour her wishes as part of *patidharma* (duty of a husband) and not spurn her. Resigned, Sage Kasyapa got up and led her into the hermitage. He satisfied her much against his wishes. As Diti lay beside him, closing her eyes and reliving every moment, Sage Kasyapa quietly left her and went out. He then bathed in the river waters and returned to his rituals. After the fire in her died down, Diti realized her mistake. She cleansed herself and went to Kasyapa to apologize and plead for forgiveness. But Kasyapa was relentless. 'Diti, I am unable to remedy the situation. Despite my dissuading, you insisted on coupling at this hour. Such behaviour is not becoming of a sage's wife. You also chose to disobey my words, so your fault is two-fold. You will bear extremely wicked demons and they will make you rue your motherhood.' Diti broke down helplessly. Sensing her desperation, Kasyapa was moved and consoled her, 'My dear, do not cry. A noble child will be born in that line and he will bring glory. Your sons will be slain by Vishnu but they will be blessed by his divine touch.'

And so the two doorkeepers of Lord Vishnu, Jaya and Vijaya, who had been children of Kardama and Devahuti, were born to Diti. They had been cursed to take birth either three times as Asuras or seven times as Vishnu's devotees. They chose the first option and met their death at the hands of Lord Vishnu himself before returning to the service of their Lord. Diti tried to delay the arrival of her children by holding them in her womb for a 100 years. Finally, she gave birth to two sons, Hiranyaksha and Hiranyakasyapa. As predicted by Sage Kasyapa, the boys grew up into mighty but extremely cruel warriors. They conquered the three worlds and indulged in many misdeeds like harassing the innocent, violation of women's chastity, destroying the hermitages of sages and insulting great souls. Hiranyakasyapa declared himself to be God and insisted that all his subjects offer prayers to him. Finally, when the world was unable to bear their torture further, Lord Vishnu appeared in the fierce forms of Varaha (wild boar) and Narasimha (half-man, half-lion) in order to vanquish Hiranyaksha and Hiranyakasyapa, respectively. They were the first of the Asuras who were doomed to lose in every battle to Devas.

Diti also bore a daughter, Simhikaa, who married Viprachitti. Their children were terrible demons like Rahu, Vatapi, Namuchi, Ilvala and the Nivatakavachas. It was one of Hiranyakasyapa's sons, Prahlada, who furthered the lineage of Sage Kasyapa and Diti. Prahlada became an ardent devotee of Lord Vishnu.

Though Asuras and Devas were always warring and the Asuras were always defeated, Aditi and Diti maintained their sisterly love and affection.

Diti and the Maruts

Daityas—Diti's children—were influenced by demonic forces because of the way they were conceived. Daityas lived in the underworld, devoid of the good things in life. They suffered insults and ignominy at the hands of their cousins. On the other hand, Aditi's children, Adityas, were entrusted with the governance of the earth, blessed with all the pleasures of life and were usually victorious in their battles against their cousins. They were recipients of the offerings of the yajnas performed by humans. They also obtained the gift of immortality with the blessings of the Trinity.

Diti was never jealous of her sister and her children. She accepted her lot with equanimity. She strongly believed that her children were not inherently wicked or cruel. She thought that it was necessary for the world to consist of good and evil, and someone had to accept parentage of the latter. Diti constantly strove to mentor and guide her children onto the right path. However, as a mother, Diti could not bear the news of death and killing of her sons by the Adityas.

When her sorrow became unbearable, she approached her husband Kasyapa, crying with her arms stretched out in a beseeching manner. Kasyapa, who knew that Indra had just then wrought havoc and killed Diti's children, tried his best to assuage her grief but failed. Finally, he suggested to Diti that she bear another child. Hearing this Diti looked at Kasyapa with hope and falling at his feet pleaded, 'I have lost my sons to Indra. How much more can I bear? Indra has been cruel and wanton in his killing. If you really empathize with the death of your children, then grant me a son who can vanquish Indra. Else I do not want your sympathy.'

Kasyapa was forced to grant her what she asked, though it was against his wishes. He prayed to Lord Vishnu, asking him to do what would be for the good of all, and agreed to grant Diti the boon she asked for. He told Diti, 'You will have your son empowered as you desire. But bearing such a son will not be an easy task. You must practise certain rituals throughout your pregnancy. Moreover, the foetus will take a

1,000 years to mature. You must be patient and devout during this period. If you fail, I cannot assure you the child's safety or the fulfilment of your desire.'

Diti was overwhelmed with happiness. Soon she grew heavy with child. She practised all that had been told by Sage Kasyapa with the utmost dedication. Several years passed in this manner and Diti's stomach grew bigger and bigger. In the meantime, Indra, having learned of Diti's request, was afraid that his father's blessings would come true. He offered to serve Diti while she was engaged in her tapas by making fire for her and bringing her darbha grass, fuel, water, fruits and roots. He wanted to keep a watch over his stepmother Diti and strike at an opportune moment. He could not bring himself to kill her but could not stop himself from planning how to destroy the womb that bore the cause of his death. Poor Diti believed that Indra was truly repentant for having killed her children.

Several years passed in this manner. Only 10 years remained for completion. One day, Diti was very tired. In the afternoon, after lunch, she sat near the door of the cottage. Try as much as she did, Diti could not control her eyelids from closing and, soon, she was dozing. However, it is forbidden in the Sastras to sleep during the day. Moreover, her hair, tied in a bun, came loose and her head fell to a side and touched her feet. This touching of the feet with the head was an inappropriate gesture that occurred accidentally. She immediately became *asuci* (impure). For Indra, this was the golden opportunity he was anticipating. Since Diti was unclean, Indra assumed a minute form and entered her womb. He destroyed the foetus by cutting it into seven parts. The foetus, being in an advanced state of development, began to cry. Indra tried to quieten it by saying *'maa ruda, maa ruda'* (do not cry, do not cry), but to no avail. By then, Diti had woken up and became aware of Indra's presence inside her womb. She pleaded with him not to destroy her womb. Indra, fearing that Diti might curse him, told her that the child that would be born would vanquish him and usurp his throne. Diti cursed Indra that he would lose the very throne for which he indulged in such heinous acts. When she finally gave birth, the seven sections came to life and were called Maruts.

Since Diti had failed to adhere to the rituals prescribed, her offspring could never kill Indra. She requested Indra to accept them as his companions, to which Indra agreed. They became Indra's companions and thus became gods in their own right, while Indra came to be known as Marutvan (the one possessing Maruts). They also helped him slay his enemy Vritra, a demon begot by Sage Tvashta.

Of the Maruts, one could move in Brahmaloka, another in Indraloka and the third is famous by the name Divyavayu and could move in *antariksha* (mid region). The remaining four could move in all 10 directions. They have control over *prana* (vital breath) and other *siddhis* (occult powers).

Thus, Diti's desire was fulfilled in an unexpected manner—she became the mother of good children, and the Maruts brought their mother fame and joy with their good deeds.

Kasyapa, Kadru and Vinata

Kadru and Vinata were wives of Sage Kasyapa and they lived together for several years. Severe antagonism arose between the two sisters, and Kadru caused a lot of hardship for Vinata and her children. Kasyapa loved both dearly and, one day, in a magnanimous mood, he asked them, 'My dear ones! I love you both very much and am very pleased with your devotion and service. I would like to grant you boons. Tell me what you wish for.' Both answered in unison, 'We would like to enjoy motherhood.'

Sage Kasyapa organized a yajna to obtain the best as his progeny. He invited all the Devas and rishis to participate in the yajna; each of them contributed towards the ritual in one way or the other. Indra, the king of Devas, brought huge amounts of firewood for Sage Kasyapa to use in the yajna. When Indra was about to leave, he saw the Valakhilyas struggling to bring a small twig from the fig tree. The Valakhilyas were parented by Kratuprajapathi and there were 60,000 of them. They were ascetics of great power but were minute beings, each hardly the size of a thumb. Indra roared with laughter when he saw them, and this angered them.

They immediately raged, 'Indra! You deride us because of our size! We will perform a yajna and create an opponent who will destroy you.' They immediately set up a sacrificial fire and began their yajna. Indra fell at Sage Kasyapa's feet and pleaded with him to intercede on his behalf. Sage Kasyapa completed his yajna and then came to the Valakhilyas who were also completing their yajna. Mollified by Sage Kasyapa's words, the Valakhilyas modified their curse saying, 'Our creation will be the enemy of Indra in the beginning, but will later befriend him. Please take the fruit of this yajna and enrich your progeny.'

Sage Kasyapa took the fruit of the yajna and came to his wives, who were waiting for him. Kasyapa said, 'I have completed the yajna for our progeny. Now tell me what kind of children you want.' He looked at Kadru first, as she was the elder of the two. She immediately answered, 'Lord, you are well aware what a woman would desire the most. I will openly ask you what I long for. Please grant that I become a mother to a 1,000 sons with shining personalities and long bodies.' Kasyapa replied, 'So be it.'

He then turned to Vinata smiling at her expectant face. Vinata modestly spoke, 'I too wish to be a mother. I would like to have two sons only but each of them must be stronger than all the sons of my sister.' Kadru, who was joyous with Kasyapa's words, did not care to listen to Vinata's request. Sage Kasyapa raised his palm and Kadru found herself holding a basket with one thousand eggs. Then, Sage Kasyapa gave the fruit of the sacrifice performed by the Valakhilyas in the form of two big-sized eggs to Vinata, asking her to tend to them carefully.

Kadru placed the thousand eggs in baskets filled with hay. The eggs hatched quickly and she became the mother of the Nagas and Sarpas (snakes and serpents). The difference between serpents and snakes was that they inhabited different regions of the world. Also, snakes were hooded.

The first born of Kadru and Kasyapa was Vasuki, and he became the king of serpents. Ananta or Adisesha is another prominent son who became the king of snakes. Vasuki was dethroned as the king of serpents by his brother Takshaka. Vasuki obtained Lord Siva's grace and served him by adorning his neck. Ananta pleased Lord Brahma with his devotion and was accepted by Lord Vishnu as his couch. He is known to have a 1,000 hoods on which he bears the earth.

Some of the other sons of Kadru were Karkotaka, Takshaka, Shankha, Kulika, Padma and Mahapadma. They, along with Vasuki and Ananta, became the progenitors of the eight Nagakulas (Naga clans). Vasuki and Ananta defied their mother Kadru when she sought their help to subjugate Vinata.

Kadru had only one daughter, Jaratkaaru, who married a sage of the same name. It was their son Astika who became the saviour of the entire Naga race, which was doomed to extinction. Using her obedient sons who were led by Takshaka, Kadru manipulated Vinata into becoming her servant. One day, while the sisters were taking an evening walk, they noticed Uccaisravas, Indra's horse, grazing in the distance, and started arguing about its colour. Vinata told Kadru that the horse was fully white. Kadru, however, said that it had some black hairs in its tail. Kadru and Vinata made a wager with the condition that the loser will serve as a maid to the winner. They decided to test it the following morning.

That night, Kadru instructed her sons to attach themselves to the horse's tail so that it would appear black. Only some of her children agreed, but the majority, led by Ananta and Vasuki, refused to be part of her deception. Kadru was livid with them and cursed that they would perish in the *sarpasatra* (snake yajna), which would be performed by King Janamejaya in the future. However, the deception was successful and, thus, Vinata was tricked into becoming Kadru's maid.

Vinata's eggs did not hatch for a long time. Years passed and Vinata bore the torments of Kadru while waiting for the birth of her sons. One day, overcome by the malicious actions of Kadru, Vinata forcefully broke open one of the eggs. To her horror, her son emerged, but he was well-formed only till the waist, beyond which hung an unshaped mass of flesh.

The child spoke angrily to his mother when she tried to take him into her arms, 'You are not fit to be a mother, you have ruined me. Now, I have to endure this misshapen body. I will not live with you.' Vinata pleaded, 'My son, I beg your forgiveness. This was not intentional. I have been slaving for Kadru for several years and was hoping for redemption. Do not abandon me. I have no one else to help me.' The boy calmed down and said, 'Mother! Please have patience with this other egg. Otherwise, you will never be able to obtain release from Kadru's clutches. Once the other egg is allowed to hatch normally, you will be saved by my brother. However, this will take many years. Now I must go.' Thus, the boy, Aruna, left his mother crying and flew to the skies. He was received by Surya, the sun god, and Aruna became his charioteer.

Vinata had to wait several years more for the second egg to hatch on its own. Her patience bore fruit and, finally,

Garuda emerged out of the eggshell fully formed. When Vinata narrated her sorrowful tale, Garuda approached Kadru and asked her what she wanted in exchange for releasing his mother from her bondage. Kadru demanded that he bring amrita from heaven for her sons. Taking his mother's blessings, Garuda flew towards Devaloka. On his way, as advised by his mother, he stopped to meet his father who was engaged in tapas. He said, 'Father, I am going to Devaloka to bring amrita to relieve my mother from slavery. I am very hungry, please give me something to eat.'

Kasyapa smiled at his son and said: 'I bless you with success, my dear son. There are two brothers, Vibhavasa and Supreetaka, who have been fighting each other for a very long time. Supreetaka asked his elder brother to divide the ancestral property. Enraged, Vibhavasa cursed him to become an elephant. In turn, Supreetaka cursed Vibhavasa and turned him into a tortoise. The two, however, continue to fight. You must relieve Bhumidevi of them. You may have them as food.'

Kasyapa then pointed Garuda in the direction where the elephant and tortoise were fighting. Garuda flew over them and picked them in his gigantic claws. He continued to fly looking out for a place to make a meal out of them. He alighted on a Rohana tree but the branch gave way because of their combined weight. Suddenly, Garuda observed that some men were hanging upside down from the branch, obviously in tapas. He quickly caught the branch in his beak and went back to Kasyapa.

One look at him and Kasyapa understood his son's predicament. He addressed the Valakhilyas, 'My son Garuda is on an important mission to Devaloka. He is born out of your blessings. Pray continue your tapas elsewhere so that he may proceed.' The Valakhilyas agreed, blessed Garuda and went their way. After devouring his food, Garuda succeeded in obtaining the pot of amrita from Indra and gave it to Kadru, thereby fulfilling his role of saviour to Vinata. He placed the pot on kusa grass and addressed Kadru, 'I have fulfilled my promise to hand over amrita to you. Here it is. Let my brothers bathe in the river and partake of it. Now please release my mother from your bondage.'

'Yes, yes, of course. Your mother is free,' Kadru said, but her eyes were on the pot of amrita and she did not even glance at Garuda. She called all her sons and advised them to bathe and consume the amrita. But before the snakes got anywhere near it, Indra snatched it and restored it to Devaloka. In exchange, Garuda obtained the boon from Indra that snakes shall be the main prey for garudas (eagles).

Garuda later became a devotee of Lord Vishnu and was chosen to be his mount. Garuda went on to be the king of birds, thus fulfilling the utterance of the Valakhilyas.

Kasyapa and His Son Ananta

After Sati's death, Siva filled the valley of Kashmir with water as it was the place where Sati and he had spent happy moments together. The lake was called Satisaras. Several aeons later, a demon called Jalodbhava emanated from it. The demon had obtained a boon from Lord Brahma that he could not be killed so long as he remained under water. He, therefore, made his abode in the depths of the lake and began to torment the people in the surrounding areas. When the Nagas and Pisacas, in the course of their wanderings, neared the lake, Jalodbhava prevented them from entering the waters. Sage Kasyapa realized that his progeny was in trouble and he immediately went to their rescue. With his yogic powers, he reached Naukabandan, near Kaunsarnag, instantaneously. He prayed to Siva and, with his blessings, cut a huge opening in the nearby-situated Varamulla Hills. Then, with son Ananta's help, he drained the water from the lake. With the drying up of water, the demon Jalodbhava lost his strength and the Nagas overpowered him. Ananta named the valley Kasyapamira (lake of Kasyapa). As time passed, the name changed to Kashmar and then to Kashmir.

Kasyapa and His Son Takshaka

Once, on a hunting expedition, King Parikshit, grandson of the Pandavas and son of Abhimanyu and Uttara, was not successful in hunting down any animal. As he rode deeper into the forest, he became separated from his retinue. Hungry, thirsty and exhausted, he reached the hermitage of Sage Samika. The sage who was in tapas did not receive him or accord him any food. Despite announcing his arrival, the sage did not respond. In a fit of rage, King Parikshit placed a dead snake around the neck of Sage Samika and left the place. Samika did not move a muscle. When the sage's son Srngi returned to the hermitage and saw the sight, he cursed King Parikshit with death by the bite of Takshaka on the seventh day from his utterance. When Sage Samika finished his tapas and learned about the curse, *adya prabhrti sapta dinaantare takshakadashtah mrutyum aapnuhi* (within seven days you will die by the bite of Takshaka), he admonished Srngi for his hastiness in pronouncing a curse on the King, 'Parikshit is a righteous king. His act of disrespect towards me was due to the influence of Kalipurusha (presiding deity of Kaliyuga). The ruler of the kingdom is like a father to all his subjects. By cursing the ruler, and a righteous one at that, you too have committed a sin.' Sage Samika dispatched one of his disciples to forewarn King Parikshit.

When King Parikshit learned of his imminent death, he realized his mistake and, in repentance, spent the week in the forest of Naimisharanya, listening to the exposition of the Bhagavata Purana by Sage Suka, son of Sage Vyasa. At the end of the week, when King Parikshit returned to his palace, he learned that his family had announced a huge reward for anyone who could save him from death by the serpent's bite. Many people thronged from various parts of the kingdom to try their luck.

Takshaka was the king of serpents and his poison was lethal. He set out to perform his duty as directed by the curse. He was very happy that he had this opportunity as he and his brothers had suffered insults at the hands of the Pandavas, and the thought of killing the grandson of the Pandavas gave him solace.

When Sage Kasyapa learned about the curse, he decided to test his son Takshaka's prowess. He disguised himself as a weak and aged person and proceeded towards King Parikshit's palace. On his way, he befriended his son Takshaka and, by way of conversing, said that he could neutralize any poison and that he was going to save king Parikshit's life to obtain wealth in return. Takshaka immediately became cautious. He said, 'I am the serpent Takshaka. Do you think you can overpower my venom? Can you demonstrate your power?' Sage Kasyapa agreed willingly. Takshaka assumed his original form and, wrapping himself around a nearby tree, bit into its stump. In no time, the tree was rendered lifeless and lay as a mound of ashes.

Sage Kasyapa used his medicinal knowledge and, with the herbs he was carrying with him, restored the tree to its former glory. Takshaka was astounded. He prostrated at the feet of the old, weak man and said, 'Pray reveal your true self. I am bound by the curse given and cannot allow it to be nullified. This is King Parikshit's destiny and you must not interfere in divine law. I will give you all the riches you want. But please allow me to fulfil my duty. Turn back and return to where you came from.'

Sage Kasyapa revealed his true self and said, 'I had come to test you, my son. I know from my powers of austerity that King Parikshit is destined to die by you. Go and do your duty.' Saying so, Sage Kasyapa returned to his hermitage.

Takshaka continued on his way and released King Parikshit from his worldly bondage. In retaliation, King Parikshit's son Janamejaya performed the sarpasatra to rid the world of the snake species. At that point, Astika, the son of Kadru's only daughter Jaratkaru, pleaded for the life of snakes and gave them a new lease of life.

Kasyapa and Danu

Sage Kasyapa sired a 100 sons by Danu, who came to be known as Danavas. They were headed by Ashvagriva. They were cousins of the Daityas and Adityas. Danavas were mostly demonic and sided with Daityas in their war with Adityas. Hence, Danavas are also considered as Asuras.

Kasyapa and Arishta

Dakshaprajapati's daughter Arishta was a devout wife to Sage Kasyapa and, through her, Kasyapa sired the clan of the Gandharvas—demigods, who were the musicians of heaven. Kasyapa's son Kubera became the king of the Gandharvas and, having amassed wealth, was known as Dhanadhyaksha (god of wealth).

Kasyapa and Other Daughters of Dakshaprajapati

Kaalaka mothered the monsters Naraka and Kalaka; Puloma mothered Pauloma. Somathi gave birth to Sumathi, who became the wife of Saagara (the Sea). Taamra bore Sage Kasyapa five daughters, four of whom started a race: Krounchi birthed the Ulukas (owls); Bhasi gave birth to the Bhasis (birds of prey); Syeni delivered the Syenas and Gridhras (vultures and eagles); Dhritarashtri bore the Hamsas (swans), the Kalahamsas (ducks) and the Cakravakas (ruddy geese). The last daughter, Suki, gave birth to a daughter, Nataa.

Other Wives of Sage Kasyapa

Sage Kasyapa married several other women in addition to the daughters of Dakshaprajapati. Each of his wives bore several children and filled the earth with various species. For example, Surabhi became the mother of cattle (cows and buffaloes); Ila was mother of flora and bore trees, creepers, shrubs and bushes. Thus, the genealogy of Sage Kasyapa reveals that his descendants are in every part of the seven worlds that comprise the universe. Muni gave birth only to daughters—the *apsaras* (dancers of heaven). They were called Maumeyas. The Yaksas sprang from the womb of Khasa. They were also demigods like the Gandharvas and they swore allegiance to Kubera.

Kasyapa and Maaya

Maaya was the daughter of Asurendran and Mangalakesi. On the advice of Sage Sukracharya, guru of the Asuras, Maaya married Sage Kasyapa to perpetuate the race of the demons. In those times, a woman could approach a man for the purpose of offspring. For example, Kaikasi approached Visravas. She gave birth to Ravana, Kumbhakarna, Vibhishana and a daughter Surpanakha. Similarly, Sage Culi was approached by Somada, a Gandharva woman, and he blessed her with a son, Brahmadatta, who became the king of Kampilya. Maaya's first son with Kasyapa was Surapadma. She bore three more demonic children. Maaya and Kasyapa assumed the forms of lion, elephant and goat while mating. Maaya, therefore, bore two sons, Simhamukha (lion-faced), Tarakasura (elephant-faced) and one daughter, Ajomukhi (goat-headed). In addition to these powerful demons, Maaya bore two lakh other demons by Sage Kasyapa.

Surapadma, the eldest of Maaya's children, obtained the grace of Lord Siva, and imprisoned Indra and Devas. After a long period, to put an end to the tyranny of these demons, Kartikeya was born to Lord Siva and Goddess Parvati. He led the Devas in battle against Surapadma. Kartikeya killed Tarakasura first, who was defending the entrance of Surapadma's palace, followed by Simhamukha. Then Surapadma faced him and, after a long battle, surrendered and agreed to serve Kartikeya as his mount, taking the form of a peacock.

KASYAPA SAVES BHUMIDEVI

Parashurama, the sixth avatara of Lord Vishnu, was the son of Sage Jamadagni, who vanquished King Kartaviryarjuna and his sons to avenge the death of his father. Parashurama went around the earth 21 times and annihilated cruel, despotic and wicked kings, thereby serving the purpose of his incarnation. Before going for tapas, he performed the Ashvamedha Yajna for consolidation of his kingdom under the auspices of Sage Kasyapa. At the end of the yajna, Parashurama handed over all the kingdoms to Sage Kasyapa. Sage Kasyapa was concerned and worried about how to allay the fear that the Kshatriyas had of Parashurama. So he addressed Parashurama and said, 'You have freed Bhumidevi from the burden of her unworthy children. Dharma (code of conduct) has been re-established. You have also atoned for all the sins that had accumulated to you. You are a Ciranjeevi. You should spend the rest of your time in solitude and prayer. Please make Mahendra Parvata in the southern ocean your abode.'

Parashurama agreed and said, 'I swear that I will not stay on earth at nights any longer and instead reside in Mahendra Parvata,' and departed.

Bhumidevi addressed Sage Kasyapa, 'I am honoured to be in your care. I will be called Kasyapi from now. Parashurama has rid me of the burden of the wicked and undeserving. But these kingdoms need to be now restored to the virtuous. Please do the needful.' Sage Kasyapa saw that Bhumidevi was distraught with all that had happened. He seated her on his thigh and sought to calm her. The touch of Sage Kasyapa was like a balm. Soothed and reassured, she said, 'People shall also know me as Urvi after being seated on your *uru* (thigh).' She continued, 'There are several worthy Kshatriyas such as Viduratha's son from the race of Puru; Saudasa's progeny Sarvakarman, who is in the shelter of Sage Parasara; Pratardana's son Vatsa, who is hiding in a cowpen; Diviratha's offspring Brihadratha, who is living with Sage Gotama on the banks of the Ganges. They are safe in different places and must now be reinstated as kings. Please seek them out and they will protect me. They also need to perform the funeral rites for their fathers and elders killed by Parashurama.' Sage Kasyapa did as directed and reinstated the worthy as kings handing them parts of the earth for governance. Thus, Bhumidevi was restored to her glorious state.

KASYAPA: AN ERUDITE SCHOLAR

Sage Kasyapa is a seer of many hymns in the Rigveda, particularly in the eighth and ninth mandalas. His name appears several times in the Vedas and the upanishads. Sage Kasyapa was a very learned and erudite scholar. He wrote treatises in different knowledge areas. His student Vriddhajivaka wrote an extensive reference book on Ayurveda, covering gynaecology, obstetrics and paediatrics, based on his conversations with his guru, and named it *Kaasyapasamhitaa*. It was later also called *Vriddajivakiyatantra*. Sage Kasyapa is credited to have written books on wisdom, dharma, music, art and architecture, which were named after him as *Kaasyapajnanakaandah*, *Kaasyapadharmasutra*, *Kaasyapasangiita* and *Kaasyapashilpa* (*Amsumadagama*), respectively, among many others.

3

Jamadagni

Aksasutradharam devam rishiinaam adhipam prabhum |
*Darbhapaanim jataajuutam jamadagnim mahaamunim ||**

Holding a rosary in one hand and kusa grass in another, adorned with matted hair, Jamadagni is the foremost of rishis and the greatest of ascetics.

JAMADAGNI: BIRTH OF A GREAT SAGE

Jamadagni is famous as the father of Parashurama, the sixth avatara of Lord Vishnu. He was an illustrious sage in his own right and is one of the saptarshis of the seventh manvantara,

---

*Visvanatha, *Vratacuudaamani*, Vaavilla Ramaswamy Sastrulu and Sons, Chennai, 1935.

Jamadagni

that is, the period in which we are presently living. He was a descendant of Sage Bhrigu, whose lineage is known for its ill-temper. Many people have been recipients of their curses, but their maledictions would inevitably result in the good of mankind, akin to the curses of Sage Durvasa.

Jamadagni's parents were Sage Richika, son of Aurva, and Satyavati, daughter of King Gadhi. He was born of an *anuloma* marriage, wherein his father was a Brahmin and his mother was a Kshatriya. Sage Richika was Bhrigu's great grandson and Sage Cyavana's grandson. After Sage Richika completed his studies and achieved mastery over the Vedas, he decided to enter *grihasthaasrama* (the order of a householder). He divined the woman who would be his wife and set out to attain her in marriage. He went to the court of King Gadhi, born from the blessings of Indra and father of the beauteous Satyavati.

King Gadhi welcomed the sage with great respect and, having seated him, washed his feet with milk and water and served him fruits. After having been served so, Sage Richika looked at the expectant king and said, 'Mighty ruler of Kausambi, I have come here with a wish in my heart. You must fulfil it for the welfare of all.'

King Gadhi replied with all humility, 'I am honoured by your arrival. When a sage who has mastered the senses and is released of all desires wants something, surely it must be for the benefit of mankind. If I can be of any service to you I would consider it my great fortune.'

Richika expressed that he had come to him to receive

the hand of princess Satyavati in marriage. King Gadhi was overwhelmed with a mixture of emotions. He thought, *'My daughter is an epitome of delicate grace and elegance. She has grown up in the midst of luxury in this royal palace. This sage is aged and has practised severe austerities all his life. What is in store for my poor daughter? How can such a match be for the good of anyone? It is however not proper for me to refuse him, for I may incur his wrath.'*

The sage, who was watching the fleeting emotions on the king's face, said, 'I have not come here for fulfilment of my body's fire. My decision to marry her is for the welfare of you, your dynasty and your kingdom. Refusal of my request would lead to insurmountable difficulties for all. If you want to test my prowess or abilities you may do so. I will satisfy you and only by proving my worth will I take Satyavati as my wife.'

King Gadhi was lost in thought and grew silent. He thought, *'To give my dainty daughter is against my wishes. Refusal would mean his wrath on me. I have to wriggle out of this situation somehow. Maybe I should ask this sage for something that would be impossible for him to grant. If he succeeds in the test, then I can be assured that my daughter would be happy, if not I would be rid of him and his request.'* So King Gadhi carefully worded his thoughts and said, 'O Great Sage! I am honoured by your request. But my daughter is a princess and, therefore, accustomed to a life of comfort in the palace. I will give her in marriage to you if you prove your capacity to keep her happy by giving me a 1,000 horses. These horses must be white in colour with one black ear. They must be of the finest breed and have the ability to gallop as fast as the wind.'

Sage Richika was able to discern the purpose of the king's request, but he accepted the challenge and left the palace on his quest. Princess Satyavati, who was a witness to this exchange while assisting her parents in serving the sage, knew in her heart of hearts that Sage Richika would come back successful and win her hand. King Gadhi, on the other hand, gave himself a pat on his back and resumed his duties, confident in the thought that he had escaped from having to agree to the sage's request.

Richika searched for such horses, but wherever he went, he was met with naysayers who suggested he give up his pursuit and return to his hermitage. However, Richika was not one to give up so easily. He remembered that there was a sacred water source, Turangatirtha, deep in the midst of Varunaloka and felt that it could be the place where he would be able to get what the king had sought. *'Why did I not think of approaching Lord Varuna? He is the progenitor of our clan and is equal to Indra in splendour and wealth,'* Sage Richika said to himself. Then, he used his yogic powers and ascended to Varunaloka.

He was welcomed at the entrance by Varuna who received him respectfully saying, 'I am indeed blessed that a person of such illustrious fame has purified this place with his footsteps.' Richika, when asked for the reason of his visit, narrated his encounter with King Gadhi. Varuna smiled benevolently and said, 'Sage Richika! I would have sent you the horses had you just remembered me. Please bathe in Turangatirtha and pray.'

Sage Richika followed Varuna's instructions. When he opened his eyes he found himself surrounded by horses. Each horse was perfect in itself, beautiful, strong and matching the description given by the king. Varuna helped Sage Richika collect a thousand of those horses, and the sage then left for King Gadhi's palace.

Upon reaching his destination, Sage Richika addressed King Gadhi thus: 'Here are the horses you wished for. Do not entertain any doubts of your daughter's happiness, O King. I am capable of taking care of your daughter and will ensure that she will be happy and content. Please give your consent and solemnize our marriage.'

Seeing the 1,000 horses, all of them milky-white but with one black ear, the King was taken aback. He had never dreamt that Richika would return so quickly and that too successfully. King Gadhi knew that he could no longer deny the sage's request and that he was no ordinary sage. He realized that Sage Richika would be the best groom for his daughter.

The wedding took place with great pomp and splendour. It was then that King Gadhi remembered the story that he had been told by his parents: once, Sage Cyavana had visited King Kusika, Gadhi's ancestor. The king and his wife served the sage with great devotion. Pleased by their service, Cyavana blessed them and performed a sacrifice there. Then, he had prophesied that his grandson Richika would marry Gadhi's daughter Satyavati, who would bear an illustrious son, Jamadagni. Satyavati would also help Gadhi obtain a son for himself who would bring great fame to King Gadhi's lineage.

When pressed for details, Sage Cyavana further elaborated that Satyavati's husband would lead his brother-in-law to excel in the knowledge of weaponry as that knowledge was available only to Bhrigu's lineage. With all this in his mind, King Gadhi bid his daughter farewell, hoping that his wife would soon give him a son—one who would bring glory to him and his ancestors.

After the marriage rites, Sage Richika returned with Satyavati to his hermitage. One night after dinner when Richika was resting, Satyavati approached him and having seated herself near his feet, began massaging them. She said in a low voice, 'My Lord, we have been married for some time now. I am very happy in this hermitage but…' She stopped and lowered her eyes, abashed.

Richika understood her unsaid words. He sat up, took her hands in his and said, 'My dear one! You have left your father's residence and all the riches that you were accustomed to and are now completely immersed in serving me. You shall have children. I too wish to have a son, one who will take my line forward. Tomorrow early in the morning, I shall perform special prayers and then you will give birth to a virtuous and great son.'

Satyavati was very happy to hear this. Sensing this to be an opportune moment, she fell at his feet and begged him to help her mother as well. Satyavati knew that her father longed for a son to continue his lineage and she told her husband about it. Sage Richika agreed and Satyavati sent word to her mother to come to the hermitage in the morning.

The next morning, Sage Richika went to the river and meditated. He returned with two portions of payasam. He knew that both his wife and mother-in-law wanted sons who would take up the mantle from their respective fathers and bring glory to their parents. Accordingly, he had infused the appropriate qualities of *brahma tejas* (spiritual essence) and *kshatra tejas* (kingly essence) in the respective cups. Handing over one to his wife he said, 'Please take the blessings of the gods and consume this payasam.' He turned to his mother-in-law and giving her the second cup instructed her similarly. He then went away to perform his daily rituals. Satyavati and her mother prayed with closed eyes and then consumed the payasam.

However, when Satyavati was praying, her mother exchanged the two cups, assuming that she would get a nobler and more virtuous progeny. She suspected that Sage Richika would have infused the best of all qualities for his own son and if she drank the contents of her daughter's cup, then her son would be the greatest king. She did not tell this to Satyavati, fearing that her daughter may not agree and would inform her husband instead. After the partaking of the holy preparation, the queen returned to the palace.

When Richika returned to the hermitage in the evening, he immediately sensed that something was wrong. He saw that his wife had changed in demeanour. Through his divine insight, he guessed that the cups had been exchanged. He was angered and told Satyavati: 'You have failed in your duty by not following my instructions. I had infused suitable qualities in the payasam. The cup given to you had *sattvicguna* (goodness) and the cup given to your mother had *rajasicguna* (energy). This was so that your mother would bear a great warrior king while we would be blessed with a saintly boy. Now, by drinking from the wrong cup, your mother will give birth to a great sage while our son will be warrior-like.'

Satyavati was aghast. She pleaded with him, 'I have not done this intentionally. It must have happened by accident. Let the qualities that you have infused in my womb be replaced suitably. We cannot have a warrior in our home. Please do something using your yogic powers to prevent this calamity.'

Sage Richika saw her remorseful face and said: 'I know you are not at fault. It is your mother who has done this. I don't blame her either. It is difficult to rise above selfishness and desire. I cannot exchange the wombs of you and your mother without your mother's agreement, which she may or may not give. I can take needful action to see that your wish is fulfilled. I will delay the birth of a warrior in our lineage. Your grandson will now be born with the attributes of the infusion that is in your womb currently. Your son will be saint-like and your grandson will inherit the warrior qualities. The power of the infusion will be held in your son and will be transferred by him to his son. That is the best that I can do, for I cannot allow the fruit of my efforts to go waste. I think God has intended for this to happen for some reason unknown to us. Let it be so.'

Satyavati was very happy hearing this. After the

appropriate amount of time, she gave birth to Jamadagni, while her mother bore Visvamitra. Both of them, through their penance and austerities, became great sages and part of the saptarshi mandala. The kshatra tejas, which was dormant in Satyavati's womb, manifested itself in her grandson Rama, who was born with warrior qualities. It was Rama, also known as Parashurama, who cleansed the earth of tyrannical and cruel Kshatriya kings.

Satyavati was devoted to her husband and is believed to have gone with him to the heavenly region in her mortal body. Later, at the request of the gods, she flowed on the earth from the Himalayas as river Kausiki for the benefit of humans. Visvamitra was greatly attached to his sister, and lived in the Himalayas very near to her, building a hermitage on the banks.

JAMADAGNI AND RENUKA

Jamadagni, as blessed by his father, was a very devout and pious person. From his childhood, he showed his intelligence and mastery of the sacred lore. His name meant 'burning fire'. His name figures several times in the Yajurveda. At one instance, he is said to have performed a sacrifice lasting four days, desirous of prosperity. When he came of age, following the footsteps of his father, he approached King Prasenajit of Vidarbha and sought his daughter Renuka's hand. The king, with his daughter's acceptance, celebrated their marriage lavishly. Renuka was very happy that a great sage like

Jamadagni had sought her hand, and she followed him to his hermitage and settled into her wifely duties with ease.

Jamadagni and Renuka were leading pious and illustrious lives. One day, they were strolling on the banks of the Narmada River. Despite knowing the difference between dharmic (righteous) and adharmic (sinful) acts, Jamadagni could not control his attraction towards Renuka in the sylvan surroundings. Seeing no one in sight, he went close to her. While they were sporting thus, Surya, the sun god, who bears witness to all actions, assumed human form and approaching them, made his presence felt with these words, 'O divine and learned sage! Pray do not fall prey to circumstances as others will follow your example and perform sins.'

Hearing a masculine voice, Renuka immediately moved away bashfully. Jamadagni was enraged at the interruption, which in itself was also a wrongful act, as interruption of a person while sleeping, eating, having sex or doing any other natural function was considered to be a sinful act. He cursed Surya to become afflicted with disease and lose his splendour. This curse led to Surya being troubled by Rahu.

Surya, who felt that he had been preventing Jamadagni from sinning, could not accept this curse quietly. He responded by uttering a curse against Jamadagni, 'I had come to do you a favour and you have cursed me instead. Therefore, you too will have to suffer. You will face humiliation and death despite the austerities that you perform and goodwill that you earn.' Saying so, Surya wanted to vanish from the place. But Jamadagni was not a person who could be easily overcome. He began to utter another malediction, trembling with rage.

At this point, Brahma intervened and mollified both Surya and Jamadagni. He asked Jamadagni to modify his curse so that Surya's splendour would be affected only temporarily, taking the form of an eclipse or when covered by clouds. Surya, in turn, gave Jamadagni two inventions so that humans could deal with his heat—sandals for protecting the feet and umbrellas for covering the head. Jamadagni and Renuka returned to their hermitage duly chastened, but this incident was forgotten as time passed. Several years went by, and Jamadagni and Renuka involved themselves in performing rituals and services.

Jamadagni and Renuka had five sons: Rumanwant, Sushena, Vasu, Visvavasu and Rama. Their last son Rama was an incarnation of Lord Vishnu and was later known as Parashurama as his main battleweapon was a 'parashu' (axe). The sons grew under the care of their parents and pleased them with their obedience, performance of rituals and study. The sons would go to the forest in the mornings to bring flowers, fruits and firewood. Then they would assist their father in performing the daily rituals, after which they would study the scriptures.

Renuka would bathe in the Ganga, which flowed near the hermitage, fill a pot with water and bring it for her husband's use. This was her daily practice. Once, the pot slipped from her hands, fell to the ground and cracked, and water began dripping from it. Renuka simply bent down, scooped some sand from the river bed and, pasting it on the crack, mended the pot. The pot held and the dripping stopped. From that day, she began creating a new pot daily. She would scoop out some sand and craft a pot in five minutes. Then, filling the newly composed vessel with water, she would return home. The creation of a pot with fresh earth and its ability to carry without it dissolving was a symbol of Renuka's implicit devotion towards her husband and of her chastity.

One morning, when Renuka approached the river, she heard some noises downstream. Without thinking, she proceeded in that direction. The reason for the clamour was that a Gandharva prince named Citraratha of Mrittikavati, wearing only a garland of lotuses was sporting with his wife in the river. Unable to control her wavering mind, Renuka stood watching the scene, oblivious to the passage of time. At a conscious level she was unaffected but, subconsciously, her mental equilibrium was disturbed. After a few minutes, she reined in her mind and, remembering that her husband would be waiting for pure water to begin his rituals, she hurried to the river bank, bathed and started to make a pot. What was an easy task everyday became an insurmountable one that day.

Try as much as she did, Renuka was unable to make the pot on that fateful day. No sooner would she shape it that the pot would collapse, becoming a mound of clay. She realized her lapse and wanted to end it all, but knowing that her husband should deal with the situation as he was her master, she did not take her life. Renuka sat on the river side, unable to return to the hermitage and face her husband and children.

Jamadagni, who was accustomed to Renuka's punctual performance of duties, divined the reason for her delay. He was infuriated. He called out to his eldest son, Rumanwant, and ordered, 'Your mother has been vilified by impure thoughts. Give her death this very instant.' His son stood shocked. He said, 'At the cost of disobeying you, I must say that such an action is wrong. I cannot commit the sin of murdering my own mother. I refuse.' Jamadagni immediately cursed his eldest son to become an imbecile and called for his second son. He repeated his order to Sushena, but his second son too refused and was cursed by Jamadagni. The third and fourth sons followed suit. Finally, when Jamadagni ordered Rama to cut off his mother's head, Rama silently picked up his axe and headed to the river. He saw his mother waiting with her head bowed. Without a word, Rama chopped off her head and returned to his father, and placed the axe dripping with blood at his feet. Jamadagni was pleased with Rama's obedience. His wrath calmed and he said, 'Rama! I am glad you are my son. I grant you anything you may ask. What do you desire? Tell me and I shall bestow it on you.'

Rama was aware of his father's extraordinary powers gained through penance and strict austerities. Rama bowed and touched his father's feet. He then knelt on one knee, looked at his father in the eye and said: 'I have only done my duty and do not wish for any boon for myself. But I do not want to disrespect you by refusing your blessings. I want my mother alive without the memory of my action so that I can continue to serve my parents for some more time. I want my accursed brothers forgiven. I want my family together again. No sin should be attached to me as a result of this act. I should be unrivalled in valour in battle and I should live long. I also want you, my father, to give up such uncontrolled fits of anger so that you may attain greater heights of spirituality.'

Jamadagni was impressed by Rama's devotion and love towards his parents and family. He immediately restored Renuka's life. Renuka fell at Jamadagni's feet and begged forgiveness. Jamadagni held her by the shoulders and brought her close to himself. He said, 'You are no longer impure. You have atoned for your sinful thought. Your place is beside me.' He then went to his sons and sprinkled some water from his kamandalu. They got back their senses once again and were no longer imbeciles. They all fell at Jamadagni's feet and, receiving his blessings, returned to their duties. Jamadagni changed his irascible temperament, and soon became famous for his virtuous character. Thus, he granted all the wishes of his son Rama.

JAMADAGNI: DEATH BY KARTAVIRYARJUNA'S CLAN

Lord Vishnu bears a mace, a lotus flower, a conch and a *cakra* (disc) in his four hands. It is said that Lord Vishnu blesses his devotees with the lotus flower and chastens them with his mace when they stray from the path of righteousness. The other two weapons are for the wicked. The conch is blown to indicate to sinners that Lord Vishnu would be punishing them soon. If such persons do not heed the warning, then, using the disc, Lord Vishnu would behead them. The Sudarsana (the cakra of Vishnu), fashioned by Visvakarma, is said to be a repository of the powers of Lord Vishnu. Sudarsana began to take pride in the power that rested in him and grew arrogant. Lord Vishnu cursed him to be born on earth with deformed, short and weak hands, whereby he would realize how powerless he was in reality. Hearing the curse, Sudarsana immediately realized his folly as he would now become separated from his master Lord Vishnu. He fell at Lord Vishnu's feet and, begging forgiveness, requested a release from the curse by the hands of Lord Vishnu himself. Lord Vishnu assured him that Parashurama would release him of the curse. Parashurama being an avatara of Lord Vishnu would thus fulfil Sudarsana's desire and help him rejoin Lord Vishnu.

The curse of Lord Vishnu took effect and Sudarsana was born with shapeless and dysfunctional arms in the Haihaya clan and was named Kartaviryarjuna. He was also called Surasena and ruled the famous kingdom of Mahishmati. He became an ardent devotee of Sri Dattatreya (the form in which the Trinity is represented as one) and, by pleasing him, attained many boons. One of the boons gave him a 1,000 arms and Kartaviryarjuna became famously known as Sahasrabaahu. Sri Dattatreya also gave him a golden chariot on which he was able to fly anywhere. Kartaviryarjuna became a mighty king and even defeated Ravana, after which he tied him to a tree and did not release him until Ravana's grandfather Pulastya interceded and pleaded for Ravana's release. All this made Kartaviryarjuna arrogant and headstrong.

One day, when Jamadagni's sons were away, Kartaviryarjuna and his retinue came to his hermitage. They had been to the nearby forest to hunt and were on their way home. Seeing the hermitage, they sought to find some rest. Jamadagni and his wife Renuka received him with all due respect and invited him and his men to rest awhile. Jamadagni, through his penance to Indra had acquired Surabhi, a daughter of Kaamadhenu, for assistance with his austerities. Surabhi, like her mother, was capable of fulfilling all desires. She would provide milk for other products such as ghee for Jamadagni and his family. She was cared for with love and respect.

With guests in the hermitage, Renuka approached Surabhi and, praying to her, obtained sumptuous food fit for a king. She served Kartaviryarjuna and all his men. The king was impressed with the lavish spread and asked, 'What is the source of all this? You appear to be a sage but possess immense wealth. How is this possible?'

The naive Sage Jamadagni revealed the presence of Surabhi in his hermitage. Kartaviryarjuna's eyes grew in wonder first and then with greed. He ordered his soldiers, 'Seize that cow and let us leave. The cow's rightful place is in my palace and her duty is to serve me.'

Jamadagni intervened saying, 'O King, do not indulge in such adharmic acts. This does not befit you. The cow supports us and through our rites brings good to your entire kingdom. Such an atrocity against her would be unforgivable and lead to your end.' Kartaviryarjuna, drunk on pride over his valour and strength in his thousand arms, directed his forces to follow his orders. Jamadagni immediately requested Surabhi to protect them and the inmates of the asrama. Surabhi produced a huge army, which emerged victorious against Kartaviryarjuna and his people. The army then disappeared into Surabhi's body.

Observing this, Kartaviryarjuna thought that he could not possess Surabhi until he killed her master. So, in a flash, he turned towards Sage Jamadagni and, raising his arm, sliced his head which fell to the ground. At this, Renuka screamed helplessly but there was no one who could come to her aid. Kartaviryarjuna turned towards the cow. But Surabhi had vanished from there and returned to the heavens. Filled with impotent rage, he left the hermitage looking as if a herd of elephants had crashed through it. Renuka began wailing and decided to enter the funeral pyre with her husband. At that moment, Sage Bhrigu appeared. He consoled Renuka and asked her to dry her tears. He then brought Jamadagni back to life.

When Jamadagni's sons returned home, they saw the destruction that had happened all around. Rama asked his father repeatedly as to what had occurred in their absence. Finally, Jamadagni told him all that had occurred. An enraged Rama took his bow and quiver and marched towards Mahishmati. On being informed of Rama's arrival, Kartaviryarjuna sent his armies comprising several Akshauhinis to the battlefield. An Akshauhini is said to consist of 21,870 elephants, 21,870 chariots, 65,610 horses and 109,350 foot soldiers, but Rama slew all of them fighting single-handedly, like a farmer cutting hay. The entire army was destroyed, the battlefield was strewn with the heads and limbs of the soldiers and the earth was blood red. Finally, Kartaviryarjuna was forced to come to the battlefield and face Rama. Dressed in splendid robes and a shining armour, his thousand hands holding a thousand weapons, he appeared frightful. Fighting ensued between the two men. Kartaviryarjuna, though a great warrior, could not face the onslaught of the fierce and angry Rama, who chopped off his thousand arms in no time. Kartaviryarjuna soon realized that his end was near. Finally, Rama killed him in the battle.

Rama returned to the hermitage to be welcomed by his parents. He bowed and took their blessings. Tears of relief flowed down Jamadagni's cheeks. He embraced Rama and asked him to narrate the details of the battle. Rama described how he razed the huge army of Kartaviryarjuna. He was still angry while vividly describing how he hacked off Kartaviryarjuna's arms and finally slew him.

After hearing his son's exploits with pride, Jamadagni advised him, 'Rama, no doubt your fight with the king was for a righteous cause. But for a Brahmin, the killing of a person is considered a sin. Moreover, killing a king, an act by which his subjects are exposed to anarchy and invasions from enemy kings, is not right on your part.' Rama was stunned but he uttered not a word. He folded his arms and bent his head. Sage Jamadagni counselled Rama: 'My son, I know that your act was not out of cruelty or any other vice but you have committed a sin. The king is considered as an embodiment of God. The death of Kartaviryarjuna will create chaos in his kingdom. This would lead to suffering of innocent people. We must mitigate the difficulties that the ordinary citizens would have to face. We Brahmins are worshipped because of our qualities of forgiveness and equanimity. It causes me distress to see that you need to achieve control over anger. Anger is the worst of the vices, for an angry man becomes blind and commits all kinds of sins. To atone for this, you need to go on a pilgrimage: visit sacred places and achieve purification of mind, body and soul. This would cleanse you of all sins.'

To Rama, Jamadagni's wish was a command. He immediately went away from the hermitage and spent his time visiting holy places. In his absence, tragedy struck the hermitage once again.

The three sons of Kartaviryarjuna could not accept the defeat and death of their father. Crazed by the desire for revenge, they became thirsty for Jamadagni's blood. Learning that Rama was away, the sons of Kartaviryarjuna decided that it was the opportune time to avenge their father's death. They arrived at the asrama and attacked the pious and unresisting Jamadagni who was performing a fire ritual. They cruelly stabbed him several times and, finally cutting off his head, took it with them as a trophy. Renuka, a mute witness to this atrocity, called out to Rama and her other sons to come and protect their father.

After his pilgrimage, Rama went to the Mahendra Parvata, where he performed severe penance and pleased Lord Siva. Rama was graced with the divine parashu from Siva, who knew that Rama would need it in the near future. He started his journey homewards when he heard the cries of his mother. He quickened his steps and rushed home to find his mother Renuka holding his father's headless body against her chest and wailing. He was aghast at the brutality meted out by Kartaviryarjuna's sons. His brothers arrived at that moment. Rama pacified Renuka and, ordering his brothers to take care of her, left for Mahishmati. He vowed that his father's cremation would take place only after he returned with his father's head.

Rama fought and killed the three sons of Kartaviryarjuna. Retrieving the head of Jamadagni, Rama returned to his wailing mother. The funeral rites were duly performed. Renuka gave up her life on the funeral pyre. Rama took an oath to avenge her grief by annihilating the entire Kshatriya race from the face of the earth. The Kshatriyas, whose primary duty was to protect their subjects, had instead begun to prey on them. By their indulgence in sinful activities, they had become a burden to Bhumi Devi.

When Jamadagni was being stabbed, Rama's mother had beaten her breast 21 times, calling out to him. Therefore, with his guru Dattatreya's permission, Rama circled the world 21 times and killed many evil kings of the Kshatriya clan.

Rama's rage did not allow him to spare even children. After this cleansing act, he gave up his arms and gifted the entire land to Sage Kasyapa. At Kasyapa's request, he then went to Mahendra Parvata and spent the rest of his life in atonement.

JAMADAGNI AND THE CURSE OF HIS ANCESTORS

Bhrigu, the ancestor of Jamadagni, was known for being temperamental. Rama, who later came to be known as Parashurama, Jamadagni's son, was a personification of anger. It is said that there is no enemy like anger. In the Bhagavad Gita, Krishna says that *kaama* (desire), *krodha* (anger) and *lobha* (greed) are the three doors to hell and one must be rid of them. Jamadagni too was a person of quick temper. However, he gained control over his anger to such an extent that he did not become angry even when the situation demanded it. Therefore, it became necessary to tell the world that anger has its own place and need. This was demonstrated by his ancestors and Jamadagni had to be reborn as a mongoose to free himself from their curse.

Every year as is wont in the Hindu tradition, Jamadagni would perform the annual *sraaddha* (funeral rite) to propitiate the souls of his ancestors and make suitable offerings to them. By doing this, one helps in the redemption of his ancestors. This rite is of importance for people so that they can pay their debts to their ancestors. One is expected to release himself from three types of *rina* (debts), namely, *devarina* (debt to the gods), *rishirina* (debt to the sages) and *pitririna* (debt to the ancestors). Debt to the gods is paid through sacrifices, debt to the sages by studying and teaching the Vedic scriptures and debt to the ancestors by begetting children.

One year, the goddess of anger wanted to test Jamadagni. Taking human form, she joined in the preparations for the sraaddha that Jamadagni was performing on that day. As part of the ritual, Jamadagni's wife had brought a pot of fresh milk to be offered to the ancestors. She had milked Surabhi for this purpose. She placed it near Jamadagni and went into the hut to bring other items. In the meantime, the goddess of anger touched the pot of milk with her foot and overturned it. She made it appear as an accident and immediately crouching on the ground, pleaded forgiveness from Jamadagni. Jamadagni did not utter a word and just nodded at her indicating that she could leave the place, the ritual would go on without any issue.

The ceremony went off as organized but when the ancestors appeared to partake the offerings, seeing that milk was missing, they said to Jamadagni: 'We are in know of the reasons for the absence of milk in this ritual. We also understand that you remained calm. But you need to make amends for this defect in the rituals. You need to realize that anger has its own place just as composure does. Every emotion is to be experienced and felt in the rightful measure at the appropriate time. When one's duties get affected, one must necessarily express the anger felt at that instance. Therefore, we curse you to be born such that you do not belong to any lineage or clan and, therefore, no ancestry—*na kula*. In such a life, you will be able to redeem yourself.'

After his death at the hands of Kartaviryarjuna's sons, Jamadagni had to go through the cycle of rebirth before ascending to the status of a saptarshi. As per the curse, he took birth as *nakula* (mongoose). He lived for many years and when he imparted the value of dharma to Yudhishthira at the end of the Asvamedha Yajna, Jamadagni was released from the form of a mongoose.

When Yudhishthira performed the Asvamedha Yajna, he fed all those who attended the sacrifice daily and gave away a lot of wealth in different forms to the poor and the needy. He also honoured the learned in various ways. Towards the end, a guard came to Yudhishthira and said, 'Mighty King, forgive my impudence but I need to bring something to your notice. If I have your permission, I will relay to you what I have seen.'

Yudhishthira said, 'You may relate what is bothering you.'

The guard said: 'Some of the maids came shrieking towards me and so I went to investigate. I saw that at the place where the maids had thrown the plantain leaves on which food had been served to the guests, there was a mongoose. This had frightened the maids. I tried to shoo it away but noticed that though it would go away, it would return every time a new set of leaves was thrown. Moreover, it would roll itself on the leaves before scampering away. I am afraid this will pollute the rituals. That mongoose could be a demon in disguise for half of its body shimmers in the sunlight as if it is made of gold.'

Jamadagni

The guard then stood respectfully. Yudhishthira was taken aback. He went out with his brothers to investigate. The scene was replayed in front of Yudhishthira's eyes. He folded his palms and respectfully addressed the mongoose, 'I am Yudhishthira, eldest of the Pandavas and king of Hastinapura. I am performing the Asvamedha to obtain merit. Why are you rolling on the leftover food? I shall be most obliged if you accept my gifts.'

The mongoose stopped in its tracks and laughingly said, 'Charity! You call this as service to the needy? O King, you do not know the meaning of dharma. What you are doing will not give you the merit equivalent in any way to that achieved by a person who served one fistful of rice.'

Yudhishthira was astonished. 'O great one, forgive my words. Pray enlighten me with the reasons for your action.' The mongoose replied: 'O Yudhishthira! You are no doubt a valorous and charitable king. But you can achieve nothing by the acts you are performing. See, half of my body is gold. I was not born this way. When I rolled over a thrown away plantain leaf, the part that touched some leftover rice made me half gold. From then on, I am seeking to make the other half into gold. That is why I have come here. But no matter on how many leaves I roll over, my body remains unchanged. This shows that none of your actions have produced the merit that you seek.'

Yudhishthira was surprised. 'I do not understand how half of your body became gold and how it is related to dharma and *daana* (charity). I have given away more than half of my wealth and you say that this is not charity. I am sure there is great wisdom hidden in your words.'

The mongoose said: 'Let me relate my story. This is about a family of four stricken with abject poverty and how they still practised dharma. Once, there was a pious householder in Kurukshetra. He lived with his wife, his only son and daughter-in-law in impoverished circumstances. They had no means of livelihood, and since they did not want to live on alms, they would starve most days. They had devised a means to keep their body and soul together such that their self-respect did not suffer. They would go to the fields surrounding the village every evening once all the villagers had returned to their homes for the day. They would then scour the earth for leftover grains and collect them. They would return to their home, de-husk the grains, pound and make a meal of them. Due to this practice, many days would be spent subsisting on water alone. One such day when all four had sat down to have their paltry meal after several days of starvation, there was a knock on the door. The householder immediately got up and opened the door to find a guest. The householder welcomed the person and seated him. Since it was mealtime, the householder placed the plantain leaf with a fistful of cooked grains that he had served himself just then in front of the guest. The guest gobbled it in no time and looked up expectantly, desirous of more. The wife served her share, followed by the son and the daughter-in-law. The guest ate everything and, then, realizing that nothing more was left to be offered, thanked everyone and was about to go out. The householder apologized to him for not being able to serve him a better meal. The guest smiled and said, 'You and your family members are indeed great. Merit is not earned by just performing charity. What is important is the state of mind in which one performs good deeds. Despite being hungry, none of you hesitated to give away the morsel that you had served for yourself. Each one of you willingly gave it to me with the thought that my need was greater. This will be told and retold by all. I am Dharma, god of death, and I came to test you. By your noble deed, you have earned a place in the heavens, please come with me. The householder and his family were astounded to hear this and even more surprised when the guest revealed his true identity. They were escorted by Dharma and went to the heavens. Due to their sacrifice and charitable attitude, the family was blessed and attained salvation. I was a witness to this. I went to appease my hunger from the used plantain leaf thrown away. As soon as my tongue touched a leftover rice flake, part of my body turned gold. I had come here with great expectations that my long wait to turn the other part of my body into gold would end but I am disappointed. Hence, I say that what you are doing is no cause for you to feel any pride of achievement.'

Hearing this, Yudhishthira, who was until then under the impression that he had performed acts of generosity and charity beyond his limits and was consumed by feelings of pride, realized the reason for the appearance of the mongoose. He fell to his knees, begged for forgiveness for his arrogance and worshipped the mongoose with humility. As soon as

Yudhishthira realized his fault, the mongoose disappeared and Jamadagni stood before him. Jamadagni blessed Yudhishthira and left the place. Jamadagni was thus redeemed of his curse and regained his earlier form.

4

Visvamitra

krshnaajinadharam devam dandam caapi kamandalum |
darbhapaanim jataajuutam visvaamitram sanaatanam ||*

Clad in deerskin, holding a staff and kamandalu in one hand, with kusa grass in the other, matted hair, so is Visvamitra of yore.

VISVAMITRA: FROM KING TO BRAHMARSHI

Visvaratha, a valiant Kshatriya king of Kanyakubja, attained the status of a brahmarshi by dint of merit and came to be known as Visvamitra. He was the descendent of Kusa, a

---

*Visvanatha, *Vratacuudaamani,* Vaavilla Ramaswamy Sastrulu and Sons, Chennai, 1935

maanasaputra of Lord Brahma. Kusa's second son Kusanabha had a 100 daughters and one son, Gadhi. Gadhi's daughter Satyavati married Sage Richika. His wife gave birth to Visvaratha who with a turn of events was born a Kshatriya possessing saintly qualities.

Visvaratha was also known as Kausika after his ancestor Kusa and as Gadheya after his father Gadhi. Visvaratha's father taught him the basics of the science of combat when he was still a child. Later, he became a skilled warrior under the tutelage of Kusasana, a Brahmin guru.

Visvaratha, who came to be known as Visvamitra, was the seer of the Gayatri Mantra and a major portion of the third mandala of the Rigveda. (About 501 mantras are directly attributed to him.) The Gayatri Mantra is found in all the three Vedas, namely, the Rigveda, the Yajurveda and the Samaveda. The Gayatri Mantra is in praise of the deity Saavitri in the gayatri metre. It is called the mother of all other metres.

VISVARATHA AND VASISHTHA: MERIT ALONE MATTERS

Visvaratha was a brave, courageous king and ruled his kingdom justly. He was married to Haimavati and had many sons. He liked to spend time in nature and hunting wild beasts was his favourite pastime. One day in the forest he came across the asrama of Sage Vasishtha which looked like a second Brahmaloka and entered it. Sage Vasishtha offered to host lunch for the king and his large retinue. Visvaratha expected homely food and wondered how the sage would provide for all of his courtiers and soldiers. The meal served was beyond Visvaratha's expectations; the dishes were many and befitting royalty, all created by Nandini at the request of her master. There were several attendants to cater to the whims of all. The horses and elephants were also fed well. Visvaratha could not contain his amazement and asked, 'Sage Vasishtha, I would like to know how a person of your means could take care of the royal entourage, and that too in such a short time. I do not intend to demean you in any way, but this hospitality was befitting the Devas. Please share the secret with me.'

Sage Vasishtha led Visvaratha to the cattle shed and pointing to a beautiful cow said, 'O King, behold the gift of the Devas, Nandini, daughter of the wish-fulfilling cow Kaamadhenu.' He bowed respectfully to Nandini and continued, 'She has been with us for several years and is like my daughter. She provides me with all my needs for my austerities—immense quantities of milk for the preparation of ghee, butter and other products required to perform yajnas and other sacrificial rites. She is capable of fulfilling any desire of a person. I prayed to her and she presented a sumptuous feast to you. This is no secret, O King'.

Visvaratha was fascinated, and thoughts of possessing such a gifted animal assailed him. After a few minutes of thinking, he said to Sage Vasishtha, 'I would like you to gift this cow to me for the welfare of the kingdom. She will be the jewel of my palace and I will take care of her personally. In return I shall give you as much gold as you want and a hundred thousand cows.'

Sage Vasishtha immediately negated his request. This enraged Visvaratha and he called out to his soldiers asking them to forcibly take the cow with them. When the soldiers approached Nandini, she ran towards Sage Vasishtha and looked at him with tearful eyes. Sage Vasishtha caressed her and said, 'Nandini, you are capable of taking care of yourself. Generate such warriors with your power who will decimate this group of soldiers and attendants. Protect yourself and all of us in this hermitage from the attack of this arrogant and unjust king.'

Nandini, being the wish-fulfilling cow, produced warriors who destroyed Visvaratha's soldiers in no time. Visvaratha's sons then rushed to fight but were killed in seconds. Visvaratha had no other option but to accept defeat and return from the asrama of Sage Vasishtha empty handed and alone, having lost not just his sons but his entire entourage.

Visvaratha spent several days in deep thought on how to vanquish Sage Vasishtha, whom he now considered his greatest foe. Finally, Visvaratha came to the conclusion that he must perform austerities and gain strength and weaponry to destroy his enemy. He enthroned the only son left as the king of Kanyakubja and retired to the forests for penance. After many years of abstinence, coupled with severe bodily hardship and prayer, Lord Siva appeared to Visvaratha. 'Arise and tell me what you seek.' Visvaratha was ready with his request, 'O God of gods! If you are pleased with me then grant me the knowledge of all weapons that are available on this earth. I wish to be the greatest of all in strength and might.' Siva granted his desire and said, 'I bestow the relevant knowledge to you. Go back to your palace and rule your subjects wisely.' Visvaratha was in no mood to live in peace. His heart burnt with jealousy towards Sage Vasishtha. Victory over him was all that Visvaratha craved, and so he proceeded towards Sage Vasishtha's asrama in order to avenge the death of his sons. On reaching, Visvaratha called out loud and clear, 'Sage Vasishtha where are you? Come out and face me.' Sage Vasishtha appeared and stood calmly facing him, waiting for Visvaratha to attack him. Visvaratha began hurling weapon after weapon towards Sage Vasishtha, who simply placed the brahmadanda in front of himself. The weapons could not singe a hair on Sage Vasishtha's body and were absorbed by the brahmadanda. At last, Visvaratha aimed the deadly Brahmastra at Sage Vasishtha but even that could do no harm to him. Instead, Sage Vasishtha was covered in a holy glow and a halo surrounded his head. Visvaratha was bewildered and left the place, shoulders drooping and head hung low.

Visvaratha decided that he needed to please the gods again and pray for power to face Sage Vasishtha and overcome him. He began severe austerities once again. Several hundreds of years passed and, finally, Lord Brahma appeared before him and gave him the title of rajarshi, but this did not please Visvaratha.

VISVARATHA SENDS TRISANKU TO HEAVEN

The Ikshvaku dynasty had a king, Trisanku, who became famous for trying to achieve an impossible goal. One day he called for his kulaguru, Sage Vasishtha, and expressed a desire to go to heaven in his mortal body. Sage Vasishtha tried his best to convince the king about the inappropriateness of his desire but Trisanku remained adamant. When Saga Vasishtha declined to fulfil his wish, Trisanku set out in search of a person who would be willing to humour him.

First, he approached Vasishtha's sons, who were great seers in their own right. They replied in anger, 'King Trisanku! Our father Sage Vasishtha is your kulaguru and he has tried to convince you that your request is impious. How could you think that we would go against our father to help you? Give up this idiocy and return to your palace and rule your kingdom wisely.'

Trisanku was annoyed. 'I am determined to enter heaven in my human form', he said, 'If you do not agree, do you think there is none else to help me? I will continue my search till I find a sage who shall fulfil my request.'

On hearing these words, Sage Vasishtha's sons cursed him, 'You are not worthy of being a king. May you become a *candala* (outcast) and roam the streets of your very kingdom, ostracized by one and all.'

At once Trisanku's physical body changed, he became short, dark and ugly. His subjects ridiculed him and his family abandoned him, he was forced to leave the palace.

Yet Trisanku was not deterred from the path of his dream. He continued to roam alone in the forest and whomever he chanced upon, shrank from fear of his appearance. Luckily, he met Sage Visvaratha, who recognized him immediately and asked him the reason for his transformation.

In Sage Visvaratha, Trisanku found a ready and favourable listener. Trisanku described his experience and ended with the words, 'Sage Visvaratha! You are my only hope now. You have achieved the unachievable—you have invincible spiritual powers and can do whatever you want. There is no other person like you. I am sure it is in your power to send me in this mortal frame to the heavens. I beseech you, show pity on me.' Now, Visvaratha wanted to get back at Vasishtha, at whose hands he had repeatedly tasted defeat. So he decided to help King Trisanku just to spite Vasishtha.

Visvaratha called some of his sons and asked them to make arrangements for a yajna. He invited all sages to participate in the ritual. All but Sage Vasishtha and his sons arrived, for they feared the wrath of Sage Visvaratha. After the rites, Visvaratha called upon Indra and the Devas to receive the *havis* (offerings) and grant the appropriate *phala* (outcome), but to his consternation, none of the Devas arrived. Visvaratha then offered the havis to agni and pronounced mantras such that Trisanku began his ascent to the heavens. He had almost reached the entrance to the heavens when Indra and the Devas counteracted with their powers and pushed Trisanku back to the earth.

Trisanku screamed, 'Sage Visvaratha! Help me, I am

falling.' Visvaratha immediately used his powers and stopped the descent of Trisanku. Now, Trisanku was frozen upside down mid-air. Visvaratha began to create a new universe around Trisanku, he replicated the heavens, the stars and the planets.

Lord Brahma, realizing that things were going out of control, appeared and said: 'Sage Visvaratha, pray stop what you are attempting to do. You have amassed a lot of spiritual power and this is no way for you to use them. You have proved your might. But remember, according to dharma, no one can enter the heavens with a mortal body. Do not deviate from dharma. Let Trisanku stay where he is. His ambition would thus get fulfilled as he need not return to earth and he will be immortal. Do not create any more objects for the new universe.'

Visvaratha paid heed to Lord Brahma's words and stopped further creation. He realized that he had lost a lot of *tapas sakti* (power of penance) and needed to perform austerities to regain it. He left the place rueing his decision to help Trisanku and prepared to start penance again.

VISVARATHA: CONQUERING KAAMA AND KRODHA

Visvaratha spent several years practising severe austerities in order to attain the status of a brahmarshi from that of a Kshatriya. His intense tapas made the king of Devas nervous since his intentions were not known. Indra was prone to thinking that anyone who performed tapas was desirous of snatching his kingship and spent his days worrying. Finally,

Indra decided that he needed to disrupt Visvaratha's penance and make him swerve from his goal. Indra sent for Menaka and instructed her: 'Menaka, you are a ravishing beauty and the pride of Devaloka. I want you to seduce Visvaratha as he is eying my throne.'

Menaka protested, 'My Lord! You are aware of Sage Visvaratha's temper. What if he curses me? Please excuse me.' Indra fumed, 'This is your Lord's order. If you dare question me, you shall face my wrath.' Menaka meekly acquiesced and left her heavenly abode.

Visvaratha lived on the banks of the Pushkara Lake. Menaka observed Sage Visvaratha's daily schedule and one suitable day awaited his arrival at the lake for his daily rituals. Seeing Menaka scantily dressed and completely absorbed in bathing, Visvaratha stood watching her, oblivious to the passage of time. After Menaka finished her bath, she came out of the waters and pretended to be surprised to see Sage Visvaratha. She bowed to him and asked if she could serve him in any way. Sage Visvaratha answered dazedly, 'Yes, yes'. And then followed Menaka meekly as she led him to his hermitage.

Visvaratha forgot about Vasishtha, his ardent desire to become a brahmarshi and his austerities. He became totally involved in spending all his time with her. Her sincere service made Visvaratha favourably disposed towards her and soon she became heavy with child. When Menaka revealed this news to him, the realization that he had been led astray from his path hit him hard. He said, 'Menaka, you have made me a householder. I need to return to my path of attaining the status of a brahmarshi at once. I will not be able to take care of you and the child.'

Menaka confessed, 'Please forgive me, I was only following Indra's orders. I have been sent by him to distract you from your penance. I too cannot take care of this child. I am a heavenly nymph and need to return to Devaloka from where I come. Please do not curse me.'

Fortunately for her, Sage Visvaratha did not lose his temper. Instead, he said 'Please leave the child in the care of a suitable person. You shall never see me again.' And without another word, Sage Visvaratha left for the Himalayas to continue his penance.

When the child was born, Menaka left the baby in the care of some *sakuntas* (birds), which carried the baby to the asrama of Sage Kanva. He named her Sakuntala, after the birds that carried her and became a loving foster father. Menaka returned to the heavens.

Visvaratha realized that he had not been able to subdue kaama and began his austerities again. He was only a rajarshi and wanted to become a brahmarshi to match his rival Vasishtha. His penance in the Himalayas was so severe that the earth began to suffer by the heat generated. The Devas pleaded with Lord Brahma to grant Visvaratha his wish and thus make him stop his austerities. Lord Brahma appeared to Visvaratha and said, 'Arise Visvaratha, you are now a maharshi. Return to your home.'

But Visvaratha was not happy at all. He asked Lord

Brahma, 'What am I lacking that I am only elevated to the status of a maharshi?' Lord Brahma looked at him kindly and said, 'You have succeeded in overcoming kaama only. There are other senses that need to be reined in; you are yet to conquer krodha.' Saying thus, Lord Brahma vanished.

This made Visvaratha more determined. He subjected his body to severe hardship while his mind stayed firm. In the summer, he performed tapas with *pancaagni*—where the person is seated in the centre with fire set ablaze around him in four directions and the blazing sun above is considered the fifth source. In the winter, he stood in an icy cold stream. In the monsoon, he withstood torrents of cold water and yet remained unmoved. All these were observed by Indra, who became very perturbed again. He, therefore, sent for his apsaras. Among them, he chose Rambha and said, 'My kingship is at stake. I am worried about what Visvaratha will ask Lord Brahma as a boon. You must distract him. I shall accompany you as a cuckoo and sing while you entice him.'

As agreed, Rambha approached Visvaratha and placing her hand on his arm spoke in a lilting voice, 'I have come to be with you. Won't you grace me by opening your eyes?' Visvaratha opened his eyes and looked at her but he felt no urge to possess her. He had overcome kaama that had ruined him when Menaka had come into his life. But another emotion overpowered him. He spat out in anger, 'How dare you disturb me? May you become a stone and suffer for 10,000 years.' The cuckoo disappeared, frightened of Visvaratha's krodha.

The next moment, Visvaratha was overcome with agony as all his efforts had been wasted. He realized that he had again been tricked by Indra. By cursing Rambha, he had lost the spiritual powers he had earned. All of this had happened because he had not gained mastery over his senses. His frustration knew no bounds, but his determination was strengthened. He decided to give up food, water and speech till he conquered his anger.

In the Bhagavad Gita Verse 3.37, in response to Arjuna's question as to why a person commits sins much against his wish, Krishna had said that both desire and anger are born of passion. They devour everything and are most sinful. They are the enemies of a *saadhaka* (spiritual aspirant) and must be conquered.

VISVARATHA SAVES SUNAHSEPHA

Ambarisha was a valiant and great king of the Ikshvaku dynasty. He was a devotee of Vishnu. Once, he decided to perform a yajna for the welfare of his subjects. As expected, Indra and the Devas believed that if the yajna is completed, Ambarisha would become empowered and might dethrone Indra as the king of the heavens. So Indra led the sacrificial animal away. When it was time for the yajna to begin, the animal was nowhere to be found. To save the king from the negative effects of an incomplete ritual, those assembled there advised him to quickly find and bring back the sacrificial animal or find a human who may be substituted for the same. Ambarisha ordered for a thorough search of the sacrificial animal everywhere, but did not succeed in finding it. He then went from one hermitage to another looking for someone who would be willing to give away their son. Finally, Ambarisha came by a poor sage, Richika (not father of Sage Jamadagni), who had three sons: Sunahpuccha, Sunahsepha and Sunolaanguula.

The king requested him to part with one of his sons and offered in exchange a heap of gold and a hundred thousand cows. Richika said, 'I want to retain my eldest son as he is the torchbearer of the family and will perform our last rites.' Immediately, his wife pulled her youngest child towards herself and said, 'My last born Sunolaanguula is very dear to me. I cannot live without him.' Sunahsepha, who was a spectator to this exchange of words between his parents, realized that he was the chosen one and so he came forward, saying, 'Father and Mother, I bow to you and accept the fate that you have chosen for me. I will go with the king.' Richika and his wife mutely nodded and Sunahsepha left the house with a heavy heart, knowing that death was just a few hours away. Sunahsepha took a bath in a nearby lake and was readying himself to proceed to the palace when, to his astonishment, he saw Sage Visvaratha and his sons coming towards the lake. He immediately ran towards him and fell at his feet. 'Give me security of life,' he pleaded. Visvaratha lifted him up by his shoulders and said, 'I will protect you come what may. What is it that you seek? Do not fear. Tell me everything.' Sunahsepha related all that had happened and said, 'I do not want to die but had to offer myself as I realized that I was not wanted by either of my parents. Please save my life.' Visvaratha turned to his sons and said, 'I am duty bound to keep my word. I want one of you to go in his place.' But his sons refused him. Angered, Sage Visvaratha cursed them. 'You are not fit to be my sons,' he said, 'In your arrogance you do not know what you are doing. May you lose all the spiritual knowledge that you have gained and wander the earth, eating the flesh of dogs.'

Sage Visvaratha turned towards Sunahsepha and said, 'Do not worry, you shall not die. I will instruct you with two mantras. Begin chanting them as soon as you are tied to the sacrificial post. I will also transfer a portion of my tapas sakti so that when you begin chanting the mantras, it will bear fruit immediately. Indra will come and save you from death.' Sunahsepha learned the mantras and, bowing to Sage Visvaratha, proceeded towards the palace.

Sunahsepha was welcomed at the palace and suitably attired before being led to the sacrificial post. There, Sunahsepha began chanting the given mantras in earnest with his eyes closed. The moment of sacrifice came and the sword was raised. A thunderous clap was heard and Indra stood there in the presence of all. 'I am pleased with you, King Ambarisha. I had myself stolen the sacrificial animal to test your steadfastness and devotion. You can consider the yajna fulfilled and you will reap the fruit manifold. I am also pleased with Sunahsepha for he has come to me in supplication to save his life. There is no need to kill this boy. I bless him with a long and virtuous life.' And Indra disappeared from there. All assembled were elated.

Soon, Visvaratha appeared on the scene. Sunahsepha went to him, clasped his feet and said, 'You have saved me and blessed me with a new life. I am indebted to you.' Richika, who was also there, came forward towards his son but Sunahsepha refused to return with him. The elders assembled there discussed the matter and pronounced that since Visvaratha had saved Sunahsepha by giving him a new lease of life, it was akin to him fathering Sunahsepha. So, Visvaratha was asked to accept Sunahsepha as his son. Visvaratha was happy to do so and gave Sunahsepha a new name, Devaraata, with a blessing: 'May you attain the heights of spirituality and become one of the mantradrashtaarah.' Visvaratha then left the palace to continue on his path to attain spiritual progress. In saving Sunahsepha, Visvaratha had exhausted his tapas sakti. Therefore, he now had to begin his journey again.

VISVARATHA TESTS HARISCANDRA

Once, in the court of Indra, amidst all assembled, Indra raised a question: 'Tell me what is the most important of all qualities in the world.'

Different answers were received. Finally, Sage Vasishtha said in a voice that brooked no argument, 'The most important quality in anyone is the firmness to be truthful.' His statement was met askance from many of the sages and the Devas present there but none openly voiced their feelings.

Finally, Sage Vasishtha's arch-rival Visvaratha scorned him, 'I dispute your assertion. No one can be truthful at all times. Indeed, I do not think there is anyone who stays on the path of truthfulness in the face of adversity.'

Sage Vasishtha shook his head and said, 'I know of one who will never swerve from the course of truth whatever may happen. He is King Hariscandra of Ayodhya and belongs to the Ikshvaku dynasty. He is the living embodiment of truth.'

Immediately, Visvaratha retorted, 'You are the kulaguru of that dynasty and it is no wonder that you feel so about them. I do not agree with your statements. You must rescind them.' Sage Vasishtha stood his ground and said, 'I stand by my assertion, I challenge you to prove that I am wrong. I am sure you will not be able to do so by any means that you use. King Hariscandra is wedded to truth. You will fail.'

No one supported Visvaratha. Sage Narada intervened and whispered in his ear, 'Sage Visvaratha! This is an opportunity to prove yourself right. You must test King Hariscandra. He will never be able to stand against your intelligence or powers and will surely belie the trust that Sage Vasishtha has placed in him.'

Sage Visvaratha pounced on the chance and said, 'Sage Vasishtha! I will prove you wrong. Let me subject King Hariscandra to a trial by fire. But you must not interfere in this. If I fail, I shall give him half the merit that I have earned by my austerities.' Sage Vasishtha acquiesced without another word.

After the court was over, all dispersed from there satisfied with the discussions that were held except for Visvaratha who was plagued with thoughts on how to test King Hariscandra. Meanwhile, King Hariscandra, unaware of all that had transpired, went about his kingly duties with devotion. He was fond of hunting and set out one day with his family and his personal guards. After a few hours of riding, they camped to rest. Shortly thereafter, two young girls sought an audience and offered to sing and dance for the king and his family. The king, pleased with their art, tried to give them a necklace as a token of appreciation but they refused it. When the king asked what they desired, they asked him to marry them.

King Hariscandra was shocked at their request and ordered them to leave the place immediately.

The girls left but returned with Sage Visvaratha in a few minutes. King Hariscandra welcomed the sage and asked him the reason for approaching him. Visvaratha attacked King Hariscandra, 'How dare you refuse to marry these women? When you can enjoy their dance and song, why can't you marry them? So what if you are already married. A king can have many wives. You must marry them immediately and give them the status of a wife.'

Hariscandra pleaded with Visvaratha and offered to gift the girls all that they wanted. Visvaratha used the opportunity. 'They are not interested in your gifts of gold. They are my daughters and as their father I ask you to give me your kingdom. Nothing less will satisfy me.'

Hariscandra realized that Visvaratha was enraged and might curse his people, so he agreed to give away his kingdom.

He requested Visvaratha to accompany him to the palace so that this daana could be done in the presence of all. This was duly done and Visvaratha immediately ordered Hariscandra to leave the palace with only the clothes on his back. Hariscandra left without a murmur with his wife Taramati and son Rohita. The people lamented at the plight of their king.

Hariscandra had hardly reached the door of the palace when he was called back by Visvaratha, who reminded him that he had forgotten to give *dakshinaa* (fee) along with daana. Whenever something is given away in daana, a small sum of money should accompany it. Now, Hariscandra had nothing else to give as dakshinaa, and so he prayed for a day's time to make arrangements. When Hariscandra tried to get work, he was prevented by Visvaratha's agent Nakshatrika (who had been appointed to follow Hariscandra till he paid his dues), who forbade everyone from giving work to him as he had given away his kingdom to Visvaratha.

At the end of the day, Hariscandra could not earn any money and so sold his wife and son to a man who employed them as slaves to his wife. The man took Taramati and Rohita with him after paying a small amount to Hariscandra, which was handed over to Nakshatrika as dakshinaa. The amount did not satisfy Visvaratha who asked for more. So Hariscandra sold himself and gave that money also to Nakshatrika.

When Hariscandra auctioned himself, to his chagrin, he was bought by a candala, a keeper at the cemetery, but Hariscandra faced the situation with resolve to do his best, whoever his master be. He was given the task of burning the dead and was made in charge of a ghat at Kasi. In this manner, Visvaratha banished Hariscandra from his kingdom, turning him into the lowest commoner, but Hariscandra did not even entertain a thought against the happenings that led to his state. He accepted all that came his way, but did not swerve from his sense of duty, first as a king and then as a human being.

The lives of Hariscandra, his wife Taramati and son Rohita turned from bad to worse day by day due to Visvaratha's machinations. On Visvaratha's instructions, the candala made Hariscandra work from early morning to late night, making him stand guard over the cemetery. Hariscandra had to help people cremate the dead and clean the place later. He had to bring firewood from the forest, dry them, pile them for cremation, take fees in the form of clothes, rice and money, and give the same to his master. He lived in the cemetery, slept on the ground and ate the worst of the leftovers from those who visited. He hardly got any time to rest.

His wife's state was no better. The person who bought her treated her worse than an animal. She was engaged in household duties and since the household was large, she wouldn't get time to feed her own son Rohita, who was left to fend for himself the entire day. At night, after feeding herself and her son what remained of the food that was cooked for all, which was usually insufficient to feed even a mouse, she and Rohita would sleep in the corner of a kitchen on the bare floor. In no time, Taramati became a shadow of her previous self and Rohita was reduced to a skeleton.

As days passed, Visvaratha grew weary waiting for Hariscandra to commit a mistake so that he could declare his win against Sage Vasishtha, but Hariscandra remained steadfast in his ways. One day when Rohita went to the forest to collect some items, as instructed by the master of the house, he was bitten by a snake and died instantly. At night, when Taramati finished her chores, she began to search for her son to feed him. After a lot of searching, she went towards the forest and found his lifeless body under a tree.

She did not have the time to lament for she was duty-bound to cremate it at the earliest. She carried the body to the cemetery where Hariscandra stood guard. He stopped her at the entrance, 'Where do you think you are going, woman? You cannot cremate a body without paying fees.'

Taramati whined, 'I do not have anything with me to give. This is my son whose body I need to burn. Please waive the fees.' So saying, she raised the boy's body towards him. In the moonlight, Hariscandra was shocked when he recognized his son. He immediately realized that the woman was his wife.

'Taramati, I am your husband. How did Rohita die? Why are you in this state?' wailed Hariscandra.

Immediately, Taramati fell at his feet crying and begging, 'How can you be so cruel to stop me when this is your own son? Please allow me to burn his body. I do not have anything to offer you as fees.'

Hariscandra stepped backward, 'I can waive my fees but I must pay my master for every corpse that is brought here, even if it is my own son. Please give something, else

I cannot grant permission.' No amount of supplication by Taramati could change his mind. Finally, Taramati tore a portion of the garment that she was wearing and offered it to Hariscandra.

No sooner did he take it than the entire area was filled with divine light. Hariscandra found himself surrounded by sages, Devas and other celestial beings. Visvaratha advanced towards him saying: 'Hail Hariscandra! You have proven that you are entitled to be conferred the title "Satya Hariscandra" by adhering to the truth in the face of all difficulties. I had challenged Sage Vasishtha when he spoke of your truthfulness. Towards that end, I created situations to see how you would approach them by staying on the side of truth. You did not fail your kulaguru and have made him proud by your actions and deeds. Since the time you came for hunting in the forest all that has happened has been my making. I herewith return your kingdom to you.'

Visvaratha then brought Rohita back to life and, with his spiritual powers, gave all three of them the same youth and vitality they had when they had left the palace. The candala transformed into Yama in front of Hariscandra's eyes and praised his dutiful attitude. The sun rose to a new morning and all present blessed the king and his family and disappeared from the sight of the commoners, who surrounded the king and took him to the palace joyfully.

Thus, Visvaratha proved Sage Vasishtha's faith in Hariscandra and the importance of abiding in truth in a person's life. Visvaratha made Hariscandra immortal and, from that day, Hariscandra was called Satya Hariscandra, and his name became a byword for truth.

VISVARATHA BECOMES A BRAHMARSHI

Visvaratha was one saadhaka who set an example to the world by overcoming all passions and attaining Parabrahman through austerities pursued with relentless determination, zeal and fervour. After returning Hariscandra's kingdom to him Visvaratha did severe penance again for several thousand years till his body became wooden. Finally on the appeal of all the Devas, Lord Brahma appeared to Visvaratha and said, 'You have pleased me with your austerities. You are now master of all the senses. You are now an exalted brahmarshi. From today you will be known as Visvamitra, friend of the entire universe'. And so Lord Brahma revealed the Vedas to Visvamitra.

Visvamitra's happiness knew no bounds. He went to Sage Vasishtha's hermitage. He did not have residual feelings of revenge any more. He only wanted to be recognized as a brahmarshi by Sage Vasishtha. As soon as he reached Sage Vasishtha's asrama, he was welcomed thus, 'Maharshi Visvamitra! A warm welcome to you! I am indeed happy to see you.' Visvamitra felt humbled and all pride in his achievement vanished. The next moment he heard the words he wanted to hear, for Sage Vasishtha realizing the thoughts that passed in his mind addressed him thus, 'Brahmarshi Visvamitra, please be our guest. There is none equal to you in the entire world. You have overcome the six internal enemies and reached this state by your austerities whereas most are born into this. Indeed you have made the impossible possible by burning your ego.'

And thus Visvaratha, a valiant king, became a brahmarshi.

VISVAMITRA: GURU TO SRI RAMA

Visvamitra intended to perform a special yajna and chose the forest where the rakshasas Maarica and Subaahu lived. These sons of Sunda and Upasunda, respectively, took much delight in attacking the hermitages of rishis and ruining their yajnas. Everytime the yajna reached the stage of *puurnaahuti* (final offering), Maarica and Subaahu appeared and poured cauldrons of human blood and meat on the sacrificial fires, effectively ruining the entire yajna. This was repeated many times until Visvamitra decided to do something about it.

With a click of his fingers, Visvamitra could have annihilated the rakshasa brothers and their hordes, but he had become averse to using the power gained through his austerities for such purposes. Moreover, he was now a brahmarshi and it did not behove him to act thus. To resolve this problem, Visvamitra decided to approach King Dasaratha of Ayodhya. There was a greater purpose to his decision of not killing the demons himself. He had been instrumental in separating Dasaratha's ancestor, King Hariscandra, from his wife. He now wanted to make amends for it by uniting Sri Rama and his destined wife, Sita.

Therefore, Sage Visvamitra went to Ayodhya to seek help from the king. When his guards announced the arrival of the brahmarshi, King Dasaratha became very panicky. Visvamitra was just as renowned for his volatile temper as he was for his austerities. King Dasaratha immediately summoned Sage Vasishtha, and they both rushed to welcome the visitor. Sage Visvamitra was given a royal reception. 'We are indeed blessed with your visit, no words can express our pleasure in playing host to you. Kindly enjoy our hospitality and provide us an opportunity to serve you,' King Dasaratha entreated with hands folded in humility.

Sage Visvamitra smiled benignly and said, 'O King, I am honoured by your offer. However, I have come here for a specific reason. As you must be aware, I am performing a special yajna, which the rakshasas Maarica and Subaahu—surely you must have heard of them—are destroying repeatedly. I solicit your help in completing the yajna.'

Overjoyed with pride that he had been approached, King Dasaratha replied, 'My armies and I are at your service. Command us.'

'No, no,' said Visvamitra, 'I do not want you or your army, I want Sri Rama, your eldest son.'

Dasaratha's heart sank. He said, 'O Sage, I may be a little old but it was these mighty arms that fought and won victories for Indra. Rama is but a child. Of what use will he be to you?'

Sage Visvamitra raised his hand, signalling Dasaratha to stop. 'King Dasaratha, I am very much aware of your valour and prowess. But I want Sri Rama—I do not want your armies either.'

Dasaratha was not discouraged so easily and he made

another attempt to thwart the Sage. 'Rama and his brothers have just completed their studies, they do not have experience in warfare. Let me accompany you. I will destroy the rakshasas and you may complete your yajna.'

Visvamitra lost his patience, he raised his voice and addressed King Dasaratha, 'Are you going to send Sri Rama with me or shall I leave empty-handed? You would have failed your promise to me. Tell me at once, I am in a hurry,' and he stood up to leave.

Sage Vasishtha, who was a silent witness till then, soothed King Dasaratha's anxieties and calmed him. 'O King, we all know what a powerful ascetic Sage Visvamitra is. Do you really believe that he needs the might of our prince to vanquish the demons? He can accomplish it in a moment. Don't you see, my King? He must have a reason for insisting on Rama. You are blinded with affection towards your sons and you are unable to think righteously. Do not worry, Rama will be safe with Sage Visvamitra. Send him with your approval and blessings.' King Dasaratha agreed most reluctantly, but insisted on Lakshmana accompanying Rama. Thus, the two brothers left the palace with the Sage.

During their first halt in the forest, Sage Visvamitra taught them the powerful mantras of *balaa* and *atibalaa*. 'These mantras will not allow hunger, thirst or fatigue to touch you. I shall also impart some potent *astras* (weapons imbued with mantras) to you. They shall prove useful to you in the future.' Soon after, the demoness Tatakaa appeared before them and gave a horrifying scream that reverberated throughout the forest. Sage Visvamitra ordered Sri Rama to kill Tatakaa. 'Please accept my apologies, I do not fight or kill women,' Sri Rama said humbly.

'Sri Rama, as a Kshatriya, it is your bounden duty to protect the innocent and slay the wicked. You are a prince and the future king of Ayodhya; you are responsible for the welfare of your subjects. So what if she is a woman? Her deeds are no less cruel. As your elder and guru, I am ordering you to kill Tatakaa and rid this forest of her.'

Without another word, Sri Rama strung his bow and shot an arrow, which pierced Tatakaa's heart and she fell down dead. Rama was *maryadaapurushottama*—the best of men who follow the rules of morality—and obedience to elders was an essential trait of his.

They reached Sage Visvamitra's asrama, where his disciples were making arrangements for the yajna the next day. The yajna progressed without a hitch until the day of puurnaahuti. Suddenly, the air was rent with the sounds of chilling laughter of Maarica and Subaahu, who appeared in the sky. They began to pour pots of human blood. Sri Rama immediately created a canopy of arrows overhead the *yajnakunda* (hole in the ground built for placing the sacrificial fire). The brothers began to hurl boulders along with choicest abuses at Sri Rama and Lakshmana. Sri Rama shot a single arrow which pierced Subaahu and killed him instantly, and thereafter flung Maarica to the distant sea. The yajna was completed successfully and Sage Visvamitra and his students showered blessings on the heroic brothers.

After the yajna, Sage Visvamitra told Sri Rama and Lakshmana, 'Janaka, the king of Videha, has announced the *svayamvara* (an event where a princess selects her husband) of his daughter Sita. Tomorrow we shall leave for Mithila, and then I shall escort you back to Ayodhya. On our way, I shall tell you the story of Sita's birth.'

The next day, Sage Visvamitra followed by Sri Rama and Lakshmana, set off to Mithila, the capital city of the kingdom of Videha. As they walked, Sage Visvamitra narrated the lives of various sages and their austerities. He pointed out Siddhasrama, the sacred place where Vishnu had lived, performing severe penance before he was born as Vamana to Aditi and Kasyapa. Visvamitra proceeded further with Sri Rama and Lakshmana and arrived at Punyaasrama situated on the banks of the Sonabhadra River. Visvamitra explained its importance to the princes—that was the spot at which Siva had turned Kamadeva into ashes. He then enlightened the princes of the heavenly Ahalya and her husband Gotama and how Indra had wrought havoc in their married life.

As they kept walking, they soon came across a deserted hermitage. It appeared as if no one had lived there for ages, yet the place was filled with a solitude that was at once peaceful and uplifting. Sage Visvamitra addressed Sri Rama, 'Here is the asrama of Gotama.' As they moved around the place, Sri Rama's toes brushed against a rock. The next moment, the rock transformed into the most beautiful woman on earth. Rama and Lakshmana were astonished, they stepped back.

Ahalya, who had been invisible to all till then, had

suddenly appeared before Sri Rama as soon as she was touched by him. Sri Rama and Lakshmana went forward and prostrated to her. Ahalya looked at Sri Rama and her eyes spoke of reverence and gratitude. Tears of joy fell on Sri Rama's feet as Ahalya prostrated to him.

Sri Rama was embarrassed and stepped back. He held her shoulders, helped her stand up and said, 'Mother, you must not touch my feet, I am like a son to you, please do not cry.'

But, overcome with emotion, Ahalya's tears continued to pour. Gotama, who had been away, returned and the couple worshipped Sri Rama and thanked Sage Visvamitra for having brought Sri Rama to their hermitage.

When they reached Mithila, they saw that the roads were full of people from neighbouring kingdoms who had come to participate in the festivities surrounding the svayamvara. Visvamitra and the princes reached the palace and were given a warm welcome. Janaka stood up and announced to the assembly, 'This is my dearest daughter Sita. She is *ayonijaa* (not born of a woman). I found her while tilling the land for a yajna, but I have brought her up as my own. This bow which you all see was the very one which Siva had gifted to my ancestor King Nimi's eldest son, Devaraata, for safekeeping. This has remained in our family since then. Whosoever strings this divine bow of Siva shall receive Sita's hand in marriage.'

There were many princes who attempted it, but none of them were able to even lift the bow. Janaka addressed the princes again, 'Is there no hero worthy of marrying my daughter in the whole of Aryavarta? Will she remain unmarried?'

Sage Visvamitra glanced at Sri Rama and indicated that he should make an attempt. Sri Rama took his blessings and strode to the altar on which the bow was placed. He picked up the bow with grace and beauty, as if it was just a feather. There was a gasp from the gathering. As he bent the bow to string it, the bow snapped into two with a loud sound. The entire assembly stood up and applauded. Sita stepped forward and garlanded the victor.

Janaka offered his other daughter Urmila to Lakshmana, and his nieces Mandavi and Srutakiirti to Bharata and Satrughna. Sage Gotama's son Saatananda officiated at the wedding ceremonies of the brothers, which were performed under the guidance of Sage Vasishtha and Sage Visvamitra. The four princes returned to Ayodhya with their beautiful wives.

5

Atri

agnihotraratam saantam sadaa vrata paraayanam |
*satkarma niratam dhiiram arcayed atrim avyayam ||**

Always performing *agnihotra* (oblation to Agni), peaceful, following all the rituals, doing only good actions and well learned, he is Atri the immutable.

ATRI: SEER UNPARALLELED

The creator of the universe, Lord Brahma, brought forth 10 maanasaputras to assist him in populating the earth, and Sage Atri was one of them. He is one of the prajapatis, one of the

---

*Visvanatha, *Vratacuudaamani*, Vaavilla Ramaswamy Sastrulu and Sons, Chennai, 1935.

saptarshis and a seer of the fifth mandala of the Rigveda. The fifth mandala of the Rigveda is called Atri Mandala in his honour, as Sage Atri and his descendants are the main contributors of the 87 hymns in it. These 87 hymns are mainly in praise of Agni and Indra. In addition, Visvedevas (all Gods), the Maruts, the twin deities Mitra and Varuna and Asvinis have hymns in their honour in this mandala. Two hymns each are dedicated to Usas (dawn) and to Savitar (Surya, the sun god) in the Atri Mandala. Sage Atri compiled material on daana, japa and tapas, which is known as Atreya Dharmasastra. Another of his treatises was the Atrismriti or Atrisamhitaa. Sage Atri and his descendants have also compiled other Vedic texts.

'Atri' means absence of the three gunas, that is, sattva, rajas and tamas. True to his name, Sage Atri epitomized the power of detachment. He, along with two other seers, is said to have put forth the theory of three strands in the *yajnopaviitam* (sacred thread). This theory states that the three strands symbolize creation (Lord Brahma and the letter A), sustenance (Vishnu and the letter U) and dissolution (Siva and the letter M). As part of *upanayanam* (investiture), after the three-strand thread is donned, every boy takes a vow to recite the primordial sound AUM/OM. When a person gets married, a second set of three threads is given to him. In certain cases, a third set is also worn by those who use it to represent the upper garment.

Once, due to Siva's curse, all of Lord Brahma's maanasaputras were destroyed. Lord Brahma then performed a sacrifice and Atri was born again from the flames of the sacrificial fire. In both his manifestations, Sage Atri married Anasuya—one who is free from envy and spite—who was the sister of Sage Kapila. In his first life, she bore him three sons, Dattatreya, Durvasa and Soma, and in his second life, she bore him a son, Aryaman, and a daughter, Apala/Amala.

Sage Atri meditated on the Parabrahman with the desire to beget progeny. Delighted with Sage Atri, Parabrahaman manifested in the forms of Lord Brahma, Vishnu and Siva and granted his desire. Soma, Dattatreya and Durvasa were born to Anasuya as *amsaavataaras* (partial incarnations) of Brahma, Vishnu and Siva, respectively.

Atri's lineage had several seers or mantradrashtaarah like Saavaasva, Avistrpurvaatithi and great rishis such as Mudgala, Uddaalaki, Saakalaayani and Chaandogya.

ATRI AND ANASUYA

Sage Atri married Anasuya, the daughter of Kardamaprajapati and Devahuti. They lived in a small hermitage in the south of the forest of Citrakuta, practising austerities with devotion. Due to her piety and devotion to her husband, Anasuya possessed miraculous powers.

Once, during the Tretayuga, there was no rain for 12 years. All the ponds, lakes and rivers dried up one by one. Animals and birds wandered in search of water to moisten their parched lips. Slowly the foliage dried up. The entire landscape turned from green to brown and the air became dry.

Despite all this, Sage Atri continued to perform severe austerities to Lord Siva. He would make a linga (symbol of Siva) of sand afresh daily and worship it. Anasuya would go far and wide in search of some water for the abhisheka (bathing god in worship) every day. It is well known that Lord Siva is *abhishekapriya* (one who can be pleased by pouring water over him) and *Gangadhaari* (bearer of Ganga). Anasuya would scoop out water from the almost-dry wells and ponds, collect it drop-by-drop in a pot and bring it for Sage Atri.

One day, even after hours of searching, Anasuya had to return empty handed to the hermitage. When she saw Sage Atri waiting expectantly for her, she decided to seek the help of the gods themselves for procuring water. She immediately prayed to Goddess Gangaa and propitiated her. At her call, Gangaa manifested herself and said, 'Devi Anasuya, behold, I am here to do your bidding. What is it that you desire?'

Anasuya bowed reverently and said, 'Mother Gangaa, you know everything. Due to the drought, I could not obtain water for the austerities that my husband has undertaken. I cannot allow his penance to be broken. Please fill this pot with water so that the ritual continues unhindered.' Smiling, Gangaa did so and vanished.

When Anasuya presented the water to Sage Atri, he looked askance, 'You are very late today. Did anything happen to delay you?' He looked at the water and continued, 'Also, this water is crystal clear and not cloudy like you bring every day. What is the secret?' Sage Atri knew everything but wanted to hear about the entire incident from Anasuya.

She narrated everything. Immediately, Sage Atri said, 'I would like to behold Mother Gangaa. Can you request her to appear here now?'

Anasuya had only to think about his request and Gangaa appeared before the two of them. Sage Atri bowed to her and said, 'Mother Gangaa, you are well aware of the drought that is hurting all the living beings in this area. Please stay here for some time and help us all.'

Gangaa immediately turned to Anasuya and said, 'The purity of your character is well known. You have the ability to do the unthinkable by virtue of your austerities. Since I am a goddess, I cannot dream of achieving such power. Please bestow me the tapas sakti that you have accumulated in a period of one year. I will stay here forever in the form of a river and I may be called Mandakini.'

Without hesitating, Anasuya immediately conferred to Gangaa the power she requested and Gangaa started to flow as Mandakini.

As soon as Sage Atri poured the pot of water that Anasuya had brought for Siva's ritual, there was a dazzling light and Siva manifested himself in front of the couple, saying, 'I am pleased with the two of you. The welfare and good of the world is dear to you and I am gratified with your devotion. I will stay here as I am Gangadhiswara and Gangaa is already here. I will be known as Atrisvara. There will never be a drought here.' With this, Siva disappeared. The suffering of all the sages, birds and animals was eased instantaneously. Water was aplenty and no living being had to suffer from thirst anymore. Forest cover returned and green and fresh foliage beckoned from all sides.

ANASUYA AND SILAVATI

During this time, there lived a sage called Mandavya. One night, a group of thieves, when chased by the king's guards, hid their booty in his hermitage and ran away. Sage Mandavya was meditating under a tree nearby and was in a state of *samadhi* (trance). The soldiers following the robbers saw the booty inside the hermitage through a window and reported the same to the king, who ordered that Sage Mandavya be impaled. However, the sage remained alive by the power of yoga.

In the meantime, a poor Brahmin called Kausika, who was afflicted with leprosy, felt that he was nearing death. He expressed a desire to visit a prostitute's house before his death. His wife Silavati was very devoted to him and wanted to fulfil his dying wish. Since Kausika was not in a state to walk, she carried his thin, worn, decrepit self on her back and trudged towards a prostitute's house.

On their way, they passed Mandavya's hermitage, where Silavati paid her respects to the sage. Mandavya asked her, 'My child, where are you going at this late hour? Who is this person with you? He seems very ill.'

Silavati answered, 'I am taking my dying husband to a prostitute's house.'

Since Kausika's foot touched him when Silavati turned to answer, Sage Mandavya cursed Kausika, 'May you not see tomorrow's sunrise.' Silavati was shocked and hurt, she silently retraced her steps home with her husband. She began worrying about her husband's impending death, and not wanting to live as a widow, finally decided and prayed thus, 'O Sun God! I request that you do not rise ever again. If I have been a chaste and faithful wife, then please accept my prayer.'

As a result, the Sun God could not rise the next morning. The world remained in darkness and chaos resulted. Indra hastened to Sage Atri and apprised him of the situation. Sage Atri asked Anasuya to convince Silavati about the inappropriateness of her action.

Anasuya went to Silavati and said, 'My dear, what is this that I have heard? You have only thought about yourself, but what about all of us in this world? Do you want your husband to continue to live when the world is destroyed? Have you understood the effects of your prayer? I beg of you, think of the world and give up this worldly attachment to your husband. Let order be restored to the world and let the sun rise.'

Silavati saw reason. Crying, she fell at Anasuya's feet and sobbed, 'Mother, forgive me. I have made a terrible mistake. I will pray to the gods to rescind my appeal.' Thus, Silavati prayed to the gods and the sun rose in the east. Anasuya then blessed Kausika with good health and a long life. He started his new life with Silavati, giving up his philandering ways.

ATRI: FATHER TO THE TRINITY

Once, Lord Siva and Parvati were discussing the sanctity of marriage and man–woman relationship. One topic led to another and Parvati looked towards the earth to prove her point with an example from humans. After a few minutes, she said, 'I can see no woman whom I can uphold as a true embodiment of chastity. I feel that this virtue is losing its place in a woman's life.'

Lord Siva smiled and said, 'Maybe you are not looking at the right person.'

Parvati knowingly looked at him and said, 'May it please my lord to indicate the woman who is a *pativrataa* (one who considers her husband as her entire world).' Parvati expected Siva to say that she herself was the best example, but Lord Siva pointed to Anasuya, wife of Sage Atri.

Parvati immediately called on goddesses Lakshmi and Sarasvati for support. They were followed by Narayana and Lord Brahma, who when asked the same question, sided with Siva. Sage Narada, who was witness to this debate, put forth his perspective. 'O Mothers of the Universe, this is not a subject to be discussed. Anasuya is definitely an epitome of chastity and purity. There is indeed none in the entire universe who can match her. There can be no question about this. It is my humble opinion that you must accept your husband's viewpoint.'

This infuriated the three goddesses and they said that it was a moot point until proven. They requested their husbands to substantiate their stance or retract it. In one voice, they made their demand clear, 'You must approach Anasuya and ask to be fed by her in the nude. We shall see how she fulfils your request and retains her chastity too.' Now, the Trinity was in a dilemma. A devotee's purity and chastity would have to face the wrath of their wives.

The Trinity descended to earth near Sage Atri's hermitage. It was nearing mid-day. They took the form of three ascetics, neared the door and, in one voice, chanted, '*Bhavati bhikshaam dehi* (Mother, give us food).'

Within a few seconds, Anasuya opened the door and welcomed them with her palms folded together. 'It would be a pleasure to serve you food,' she said. 'Please make yourselves comfortable. I will bring food for you.' She requested them to come inside and be seated.

Lord Brahma said, 'Thank you for offering us food but we are bound by some rules. We can accept alms only if you will be able to satisfy our rules. Is your husband at home? You may need to seek his permission to do what we say.'

Anasuya replied, 'My husband Sage Atri is away at the moment. However, I cannot allow you to go away from my door without appeasing your hunger. Please tell me your conditions. I will prepare food accordingly.'

Vishnu said, 'Can you give us your word that you will do as we bid you?' Without a moment's hesitation, Anasuya nodded in the affirmative. Siva said, 'You must feed us without your clothes, in the nude. Only then can we consume the food that you serve.' Anasuya was shaken for a second but recovering quickly, she prayed to her husband and replied, 'Please come in. I will serve you as per your condition.'

The Trinity seated themselves. Anasuya went into the kitchen and prayed to the Parabrahman, 'My chastity and loyalty to my husband has always been true. It is my very identity. Please guide me in this trying time.' She then brought out holy water and sprinkled a few drops on the three ascetics.

An amazing thing occurred: the ascetics turned into infants. Anasuya removed her saree and breastfed them one by one with milk that poured out miraculously. She then created cradles and laid the babies in them. She rocked the babies and sang lullabies to put them to sleep. She was delighted with the antics of the three tots.

Many days passed and Anasuya spent her time with the three babies, bathing and clothing them, feeding them and enjoying motherhood afresh. Sage Atri returned from his journey and was pleasantly surprised to see three babies playing around. He asked Anasuya about it and she narrated the entire incident to him in detail. He smiled knowingly but did not make any comment.

In the meantime, Parvati, Lakshmi and Sarasvati, who were witnessing all this from the heavens, were taken aback at Sage Atri's response to the situation. They came down to earth and when Sage Atri was engrossed in his morning rituals and Anasuya was in the kitchen, approached the babies and said, 'O Lords, please take your original form and return with us. How long can the universe survive without you?'

Lord Brahma answered, 'We are helpless tots. We cannot

regain our form unless Anasuya wills it.'

Parvati, Lakshmi and Sarasvati entreated, 'Please do not say so. We have realized our mistake. We accept that we were wrong. You must come back immediately. Anasuya is truly a great woman.'

Vishnu said, 'It is good that you have realized the truth in our words. Sage Narada was only trying to prove this. But Anasuya and her husband must release us. Only then can we return.' Siva then gave the answer that was being sought, 'You must appear before the couple, tell them all and beg Anasuya for the return of your husbands. That is the only way out.'

Parvati, Lakshmi and Sarasvati appeared before Anasuya and Sage Atri, who prostrated at their feet in wonderment. Parvati said, 'Sage Atri, your wife has won us over with her purity and chastity. We have come to ask for *bhikshaa* (alms) from her.'

Sage Atri said, 'O Mothers of the Universe, our home has been purified by your very presence. What do we have to offer to you? Pray tell us and we will be honoured to do your bidding.' Parvati stepped forward and related the entire discussion, Sage Narada's words and how the three of them had insisted that their husbands test Anasuya's chastity. Sage Atri said, 'But where are your husbands? I don't see them here. They are not in my hermitage. You must be mistaken.'

Lakshmi implored Anasuya, 'We doubted you. Now with the power of your penance our husbands are mere toddlers at your feet. Please give our husbands back.'

At their behest, Anasuya sprinkled holy water from her

husband's kamandalu while meditating on the Parabrahman and prayed that the Trinity return to their original forms. Lo and behold, Lord Brahma, Vishnu and Siva stood in their presence. Flowers showered from the skies. The Trinity declared, 'You are indeed Sati Anasuya, and the three worlds will know you as such. We wish to grant you a boon. Ask what you want.'

Sage Atri and Sati Anasuya bowed and the latter said, 'I have enjoyed your antics as toddlers and I wish to experience motherhood again. Please grant me the opportunity. I wish to be a mother to you. Grant me children and be born unto me.' Thus, the Trinity blessed them with three sons: Dattatreya, Soma and Durvasa.

Dattatreya was the eldest of the three sons. His name is made of two words: *datta* (given) and *aatreya* (son of Atri). He had three faces representing the Trinity and three pairs of hands, each pair holding the symbols of the respective gods of the Trinity, but a single body. He was always accompanied by four dogs symbolizing the Vedas and a cow, which represents Mother Earth. The creator, preserver and destroyer are all manifested in Dattatreya's personality. Dattatreya left his home and wandered all over the world as an *avadhuuta*—an ascetic who has given up all attachment to worldly objects. When Atri and Anasuya felt the absence of a child in the house, they craved for one again.

Thus, Soma (moon) was born to the couple. The entire ninth mandala of the Rigveda is devoted to his praise. He is the presiding deity of the soma creeper, the juice of which is often used in sacrifice as oblation and also consumed by the participants. When he came of age, Dakshaprajapati married 27 of his daughters (who symbolize the 27 nakshatras) to Soma. However, Soma took more interest in Rohini and neglected the others. This angered them and they went and complained to their father. Moved by his daughters' plight, Daksha cursed Soma to die. To escape from the curse, Soma prayed to Siva. His parents and his wives, who by then had realized their folly, also joined him in his prayers to Siva. Siva was pleased but he could not retract Daksha's curse, and so he modified it slightly. Accordingly, when Soma waxes in strength it is the bright half of the month and when he wanes it is the dark half. Also, Siva wore him on his head as a crescent.

Then Atri and Anasuya had another child who was named Durvasa: one who is difficult to live with. He is said to be a partial incarnation of Siva. He is known to be easily pleased but also quickly angered. There are instances of him giving boons when pleased, as in the case of Kunti, to whom he gave mantras to invoke any deity and have a son after she served him diligently. That is how the Pandavas were born to Kunti and her husband Pandu.

On another occasion, pleased by Duryodhana's royal hospitality, he agreed to Duryodhana's suggestion to visit the Pandavas, who were in exile in the forest. He demanded of Yudhishthira that he and his large group of disciples be fed. The Pandavas had just finished their mid-day meal. The *akshayapaatra* (inexhaustible vessel) given by Surya to provide them daily food had been cleaned by Draupadi and there was nothing left. The Pandavas began to tremble that Durvasa might curse them. Draupadi brought the akshayapatra to him to show that it had been used and washed clean. Since the vessel could not be used for the same meal again, Draupadi did not know how to feed Durvasa and his disciples. Krishna picked up a grain of rice sticking to the bottom of the vessel and ate it expressing satisfaction. That very moment, Durvasa and his disciples burped. They felt that they could not eat even a morsel and hence disappeared from the place. Thus, the Pandavas were protected by the divine intervention of Krishna.

Durvasa was also responsible for the banishment and subsequent demise of Lakshmana in the Ramayana by forcing him to go against Rama's command. Rama was in conversation with Kaala (time) and Durvasa had come to remind him that his life's purpose was over; it was time for him to return to Vaikuntha. Lakshmana had been strictly ordered by Rama not to permit anyone to enter. But being threatened by Durvasa's curse, Lakshmana allowed the sage to enter the room. Since he disobeyed Rama, Lakshmana left the palace and the world.

ATRI'S DAUGHTER APALA

Apala was the only daughter of Sage Atri and Sati Anasuya. She was a *brahmavaadinii* (a woman who speaks about Parabrahman) in her own right. Accordingly, Apala underwent upanayanam, kept the Vedic fires, studied the

Vedas under her father and survived by begging for food. After her *samaavartana* (valedictory rite at the end of Vedic studies), she got married and lived with her husband. After a few years, she was afflicted with a serious skin disease. When her husband learned of her ailment, he abandoned her and went away on a pilgrimage. Apala returned to her father's home. Sage Atri and Anasuya were saddened by Apala's state and did their best to console her.

Sage Atri built a separate hut for her and she began living there. She spent her time in austerities and avoided contact with others in the hermitage. She prayed incessantly to obtain succour from her disease.

One day, she was returning from the river after performing her daily rituals on the river bank when she met an old man hobbling towards the river. She went to assist him but, remembering her disease, stopped herself. The old man said, 'Please help me. Can you grind this grass and apply it on my fingers which are diseased? Even drinking a drop of this juice will cure one of all diseases.' He held forward a bunch of soma grass.

Apala saw his fingers were just stubs and he was suffering from the same disease as she was. Her heart leaped with hope. She took the soma grass and placing them on a nearby rock, tried to extract juice from it but couldn't. She then chewed the grass and spit the juice from it into a cup made from a banyan leaf. She handed over the cup containing the soma juice to the old man, resisting the temptation to drink it to cure her own illness.

No sooner had the old man taken the cup in his hand that, in his place, Lord Indra stood in front of Apala. Immediately, she fell at his feet saying, 'Forgive me Lord, I failed to recognize you. You know the cure for all illnesses; please cure me of this disease that has robbed me of marital happiness.'

Indra smiled and said, 'You did not drink one drop of the juice even when you were chewing the soma grass. I had come here to test you. This cup of juice is for you. Drink this soma juice and be blessed with health and vitality.' Indra handed over the cup back to her and vanished. Apala drank the juice and was immediately transformed into her original healthy state. She rushed to the hermitage to share her joy with her father and mother. Shortly thereafter, her husband returned from his pilgrimage and she left with him.

ATRI AND SRI RAMA

Due to Dasaratha's boons to Kaikeyi, Sri Rama had to go to the wilderness in exile for 14 years. His wife Sita and brother Lakshmana accompanied him. On their way, they halted at Sage Bharadvaja's asrama, and from there, proceeded to Citrakuta as per Bharadvaja's advice.

On their way, they met many sages who apprised Sri Rama of the rakshasas, Khara and Dushana, who were harassing people and making their lives miserable. Sri Rama promised them succour and moved ahead. On their way, they came across the hermitage of Sage Atri and Anasuya. Their hut was near a lake that contained crystal clear water and was inhabited by many swans, geese and cranes. The lake was filled with pink lotuses.

They were warmly welcomed by the saintly couple. After milk and fruits were served to the guests, Atri began talking: 'Prince Sri Rama, I want you to know my wife Anasuya, who has stood by me for all these years. She was responsible for bringing rain and for protecting families during a 12-year-long drought. She, through her piety and meritorious deeds, brought Gangaa down to earth, who now flows here as Mandakini.' Atri then addressed Sita and said, 'Anasuya is like a mother to you. Please spend some time with her. That would make her happy.'

Sita promptly went with Anasuya to the neighbouring room after having received Sri Rama's permission. She paid her respects and enquired about Anasuya's health.

Anasuya seated Sita beside her on a mat and, taking her delicate hand in her wrinkled palms, began speaking, 'I have heard from many about your svayamvara but wish to hear about it from you. Can you tell me the sequence of events in detail so that I can visualize them?' Sita began her narrative from her first interaction with Sri Rama in the palace garden of Mithila, when she started praying that he wins in the svayamvara, the decorations of the marriage hall, the several princes who had assembled and Ravana's failure to string the bow. She described every incident till Sri Rama's breaking of the bow, much to the joy of Anasuya, who had tears in her eyes by the end of it.

Anasuya then said: 'You are now married and must live

with Sri Rama for the rest of your life. One must follow one's husband in whatever path he takes. It is not important whether he is rich or poor, he must be worshipped as god by the wife. That is the only path for a woman to reach the heavens. Women who dominate their husbands commit wrong actions and move away from the path of dharma. Those who obey their husbands do good deeds and reach svarga (heaven). This way you will remain happy and content throughout your life.'

Sita was touched by Anasuya's words. She replied: 'I am honoured to receive your blessings and guidance. I had heard similar words of advice from my parents during the wedding ceremonies and know that these are the qualities of a pativrataa. Even if my husband is not a good person, I must follow him. However, I am extremely lucky to have received Sri Rama as my husband. He treats queens Kaikeyi and Sumitra with as much love and affection as he treats his own mother Queen Kausalya. He is the epitome of goodness and respects all women like his own mother. I cannot fail such a person in any manner. *Patisevaa* (serving the husband) is the foremost dharma for me. I also know the reason why you are called Sati Anasuya. I shall always follow your advice.'

Hearing Sita's words, Anasuya kissed her on her forehead. 'I have achieved a lot of spiritual sakti by my tapas. I now wish to offer you a boon of your desire.'

Sita smiled and replied, 'You have given me all that I need by your words on the importance of *satiitva* (chastity). I do not want anything else'.

Pleased with her reply, Anasuya gave her some ornaments,

clothes, flowers, perfumes and pastes. 'These will add to your lustre and help you maintain your health and vitality. You are to Sri Rama what Lakshmi is to Vishnu. It is now sunset. Sage Atri has finished his agnihotra. So please go and serve your husband. But before you take leave, please wear all that I have given you. I would like to see you fully attired.' Sita dressed herself as per Anasuya's request and after paying her respects went to Sri Rama's presence and told him all that had transpired. Sri Rama and Sita stayed there for the night.

In the morning, Sri Rama, Lakshmana and Sita left after the morning rituals. Atri described the way to the Dandakaranya forest, warning them of the *narabhakshakas* (human eaters) and rakshasas who waylaid travellers. Atri requested Sri Rama to redeem all of them from these wicked demons who had made the life of those who lived there a living hell. During his stay in Pancavati, Sri Rama single-handedly decimated the armies of rakshasas headed by Khara and Dushana at a place called Janasthana. Sri Rama also killed the rakshasas Viradha and Kabandha, the latter by tearing away his arms.

ATRI SHOWS THE WAY TO PARABRAHMAN

In the late Vedic ages, people were classified based on their guna and karma into two prominent *varnas* (groups) only—brahmavarna and *kshatravarna* (the learned and the protectors). The rest of the society was one big class. In those days, it was possible to move between these two varnas.

According to the Vedas, the path to the highest knowledge

of Parabrahman is extremely difficult and requires discipline of body, mind and intellect. Any person, irrespective of his birth or origin, who dedicates himself to a life of such austerity, is said to be of the brahmavarna. There are several examples of those who attained knowledge of the Parabrahman and were recognized as belonging to the brahmavarna despite being born into families that pursued other activities. Visvamitra, though born a king, attained the status of brahmarshi by dint of severe tapas alone. He is attributed to having realized the Parabrahman by chanting of the Gayatri Mantra, which is the most sacred hymn for all Hindus.

Sage Atri was among the first to define the path to the Parabrahman. In the Smriti composed by Sage Atri, he clearly states that by birth, every man is a Sudra or an ignorant person. Only through certain *samskaras* (sacraments) does a person become *dvija* (twice born). By the study of the scriptures, the person becomes a *vipra* (scholar in Vedas) and by realization of the Parabrahman, the person finally attains the status of being part of brahmavarna.

In the Bhagavad Gita, Krishna has affirmed the same to Arjuna. In the later stages of the Dvaparayuga, the two-varna system had become a four-varna system, where people were classed into four categories—Brahmin, Kshatriya, Vaishya and Sudra. This was done not only on the basis of guna and karma in the individuals, but also on the basis of the families into which they were born. Further, the varna system began to be called as the jati system, in which people were categorized on the basis of the professions they pursued.

However, even today, Sage Atri's definition shows the path to the Parabrahman.

ATRI PUNISHES INDRA

Atri and Anasuya were an ideal couple and complimented each other in all respects. Both devoted all their time to austerities. Sage Atri spent most of his time away from the hermitage practising asceticism while Anasuya performed rituals at home. However, with the coming of children, their way of life changed. When Sage Atri wanted to leave the asrama for penance, Anasuya reminded him of his responsibility towards their children and asked him to obtain wealth to foster their needs. Sage Atri decided to approach King Prithu and set out for his kingdom.

When Sage Atri reached King Prithu's palace, he was accorded a warm welcome by the King. He said, 'O King! I am pleased with your reception. I am now a householder with a family to provide for. I require cattle and land to take care of their needs, so I have come to appeal to your generosity.'

King Prithu magnanimously replied, 'O Great Sage! My humble kingdom has been sanctified by your arrival. I would be more than happy to be of service to you. My entire wealth and kingdom are at your disposal. However, I am in a quandary and in great need of guidance, pray hear me out.'

Sage Atri acquiesced and King Prithu began thus: 'I made a *sankalpa* (resolve) to perform the Asvamedha Yajna. Preparations have already begun and the date is approaching fast. However, the safety of the horse that will be used in the yajna is the cause of my worry. I am strongly inclined to believe that Indra does not want me to succeed in completing this yajna and will try his utmost to steal the horse. I have assigned my son to guard it. But he is a young boy. Therefore, I request you to accept the responsibility of ensuring that the horse is not stolen and my yajna is completed successfully.'

Sage Atri agreed to his request. The yajna began and the sacrificial horse was protected by Vijitasva, the son of Prithu. As suspected by King Prithu, Indra stealthily led the horse away to the skies. Prithu's son who noticed this was shocked that it was the king of Devas himself. He was in a dilemma if he should foil Indra or not and turned towards Sage Atri for counsel. When asked by Prithu's son what he ought to do, the sage, who was observing the scene keenly, advised him thus, 'Anyone who becomes or causes an obstacle to the practise of dharma is punishable, even if it is the king of Devas himself. Aim your arrows at the person leading the horse away and bring back the horse.'

Vijitasva followed Sage Atri's counsel and shot his arrows at Indra, wounding him deeply. An injured Indra abandoned the horse and made his escape. But even before the horse could be brought back to earth, Indra returned and tried to whisk it away again, but this time he was invisible. Sage Atri absorbed Indra's powers and made him visible. Prithu's son attacked Indra again and chased him away. The horse was brought back safely and the yajna proceeded without any further hindrance under Sage Atri's direction.

After the completion of the Asvamedha Yajna, King Prithu addressed all the assembled people and thanked everyone for their help and cooperation. He specifically praised Sage Atri for his role in saving the horse. Sage Atri immediately returned his compliments: 'King Prithu, I have not done anything out of the way. I had come here for wealth and was happy to be of assistance in a small way. You have completed the Asvamedha Yajna successfully and are now equal to Indra who, though king of Devas, came here as an ordinary thief to thwart your sacrifice fearing that it would bestow you with powers beyond his own. You maintained equilibrium in this critical time and fulfilled your dharma towards the people.'

Many other sages who were there felt envious hearing their mutual praise. Sage Gotama took the lead and said, 'Sage Atri! Is it not wrong on your part to praise a king thus? Is it not against dharma?' Sage Atri assured Sage Gotama that it was not so, and turning to the assembled, asked them to decide if he was wrong.

The sages could not come to a decision and so approached Sanatkumara, a maanasaputra of Lord Brahma. Sanatkumara instantly replied: 'Sage Atri has not erred in any manner. He is dharma personified. Vishnu resides in all beings but a king represents Lord Vishnu himself. A king has in him parts of gods like Indra, Vayu, Yama, Surya, Agni, Varuna, Candra and Kubera and is, therefore, to be highly venerated. King Prithu has performed the Asvamedha Yajna successfully and can definitely be equated to Indra.'

All the sages including Sage Gotama accepted

Sanatkumara's ruling and apologized to Sage Atri. Sage Gotama embraced him, saying, 'My intention was only to bring out the subtleties of dharma for all to know and understand and I have succeeded in it.'

ATRI SAVES DRONA

In the great war of the Mahabharata, after the death of Bhishma, Drona was made the commander of the Kaurava armies. On the eleventh and twelfth days, Drona devised tactics to capture Yudhishthira alive in an attempt to make the Pandavas surrender. Failing in this, the next day, Drona planned a strategic formation called the Cakravyuha and succeeded in trapping and killing Abhimanyu, Arjuna's son. Because of Drona's strategies and martial prowess, on the fourteenth day of the war, many lives from the Pandava side were lost in the battle, and the disheartened Pandavas planned the death of Drona. As advised by Krishna, on the fifteenth day, Yudhishthira announced in Drona's presence that Asvathama had been killed by Bhima, adding that it was an elephant in an undertone. Drona's son's name was Asvathama. As everyone knew that Yudhishthira was the apostle of truth, Drona mistook Yudhishthira's words and grief overtook him.

At this point, Sage Atri, leading the saptarshis, intervened as the saptarshis realized that Drona in his anger would be unstoppable and carnage beyond proportions would be the result. Sage Atri and the others addressed Drona from the skies, 'Drona, you are without doubt, a great warrior. But you are a Brahmin. And the Brahmin's dharma is to study and to teach. You know that dharma is on the side of the Pandavas, you should have excused yourself from the war. But you have participated in order to prove your loyalty. You have taken up arms, which is against your dharma. We implore you to give up your weapons and stop killing innocents.'

Sage Bharadvaja added, 'My son, please listen to us and save your soul from the endless cycle of births and deaths.' Drona's grief subsided and his anger was mollified. He placed his weapons aside. He saluted the saptarshis and sat in a yogic posture. He removed all feelings of *raga* (passion) and *dvesha* (hatred), and filled his mind with pure and sublime thoughts. Concentrating on the Parabrahman, he closed his eyes and began to meditate. His soul left his body before Drishtadyumna chopped his head off. Thus, it was Sage Atri's kind nature that enabled Drona to make amends for his wrong actions, in the last moments of his life.

6

Bharadvaja

jatilam tapasaasiddham yajnasuutraakshadhaarinam |
kamandaludharam nityam bharadvaajam natosmyham ||*

Bharadvaja, of matted hair, accomplished in penance, wearing sacrificial thread, holding a rosary and a kamandalu in hand, is worthy of respect.

BHARADVAJA: UNWANTED SON OF BRIHASPATI

Sage Bharadvaja, unlike some other sages, was not a maanasaputra of Lord Brahma. His birth was not welcomed by either of his parents. He became famous for his quest for

---

*Visvanatha, *Vratacuudaamani*, Vaavilla Ramaswamy Sastrulu and Sons, Chennai, 1935.

wisdom, and ultimately attained his lofty status by sheer dint of his austerities. He was an embodiment of Vedic wisdom and science. He became one of the saptarshis and worked at spreading knowledge and peace throughout his life.

Sage Angirasa had three sons—Utathya, Brihaspati and Samvarta. All of them were great seers. Brihaspati was the exalted preceptor of Devas. Once, his elder brother Utathya was away on a pilgrimage, unaware that his wife Mamataa was pregnant. At that time, Brihaspati went to meet Utathya, and though Mamataa was alone, she welcomed her brother-in-law and seated him. She told him, 'Sir, I am unable to serve you anything. Your brother is away and I am heavy with child. Kindly excuse me.' Brihaspati smiled at her graciously.

But suddenly his mind was filled with devious thoughts. His mind ordered him to leave immediately but his lust overcame his resolve and he revealed his desire to Mamataa. She was horrified to hear that and fell at his feet wailing, 'Sir, how can you even entertain such a thought towards me? I am the wife of your elder brother and according to the social system, occupy the place of your mother. You must treat me with respect that is appropriate of this relation. Moreover, I am pregnant with your brother's seed. Even having such thoughts would amount to a heinous sin. Please go away'.

Her appeal fell on deaf ears. Brihaspati shamelessly pulled her up by her arms and hugging her tightly began to shower kisses. Suddenly Brihaspati was chastened by a tiny voice which implored, 'I am a fully formed foetus and have completely occupied my mother's womb. There is no place for another. Please leave my mother alone and go away.'

Brihaspati was taken by surprise and, releasing Mamataa, moved a step back. When he realized that the voice came from Mamataa's womb, he was infuriated. 'How dare you interrupt my moments of pleasure! All creatures are entitled to carnal pleasure and any interruption then is a sin by itself. I curse that you be enveloped in darkness forever.' This caused the baby to be born blind later and so he was named Dirghatamas (one in perpetual darkness).

Brihaspati then forced himself on Mamataa and satisfied his craving. Bharadvaja was immediately born of this ignominious union. The foetus inside Mamataa's womb pushed out this newly created baby and it fell on the ground beside the prone and weeping Mamataa. Brihaspati did not give the child a second glance and prepared to leave. Mamataa sat up and her rage erupted, 'I do not want this baby of yours and you cannot force me to nourish it. Take it away from my sight.'

Brihaspati realized the enormity of the sin that he had committed. 'How could I commit such a heinous sin? Me, the preceptor of the Devas! The wisest in all the three worlds!' This thought haunted him until he remembered that he had been cursed to violate his brother's wife by Sukracharya, the guru of Asuras. Sometime earlier, Brihaspati had connived to convince the demons in getting Sukracharya evicted from *patalaloka* (underworld) and this had led to the curse. He was assailed by thoughts on how he should repent for this sin.

While lost in such thoughts, he was brought back to the situation by a small voice saying, 'You have violated my mother, and brought me into this world where I shall have to live an orphan. May your wife also cause sorrow to you by choosing to abandon you for another man.' His newly born child had uttered this curse. Brihaspati was aghast. He backed out from there afraid that Mamataa's ire would turn into another curse.

Mamataa turned towards the baby. His face was luminous and his eyes sparkled. Mamataa took him in her arms and went towards the banks of the Ganga River flowing nearby. She placed the child on the shore and prayed, 'Mother Gangaa, please take care of this child. I cannot take the onus of bringing him up and, hence, I am leaving him to your care. He is born of two fathers, but now is unwanted by both.' She left the river bank with tears flowing down her cheeks, her body racked with pain, both physical and mental.

The child lay blissfully unaware of its state. Incidentally, at that moment, the Maruts were flying in the sky as is their wont. They chanced upon the child and descended on the banks of the river and approached the child. They divined that this was Brihaspati's offspring and the grandson of Sage Angirasa. The Maruts collected the child and took him with them. They brought him up with care and taught the boy everything they knew.

BHARADVAJA: QUEST FOR ETERNAL KNOWLEDGE

All the rishis engage themselves in acquiring knowledge, but Sage Bharadvaja's unquenchable thirst for knowledge was unparalleled. From his birth, his inquisitive mind constantly amazed all who interacted with him. He was always seeking answers to his questions. The Maruts had taught him all that they knew, but they could not satisfy him. Bharadvaja was determined to devote his entire life to the study of Vedas. He studied, he travelled and held discussions with several renowned sages and scholars. At the end of a lifespan, that is, a 100 human years, Bharadvaja was still seeking answers. Finally, the Maruts told him, 'Dear one, Indra alone can grant you the knowledge you seek. Appease the lord of Devas and you will achieve your purpose.' Yet, they were surprised when Bharadvaja took their words seriously and left for the forests to perform penance.

Bharadvaja performed severe austerities. Indra was impressed with his fervour and, appearing before him, said, 'Bharadvaja, open your eyes. I am here to grant your wish. What do you seek from me?'

Bharadvaja was delighted at Indra's appearance and unhesitatingly said, 'O Lord, I seek knowledge.'

Indra replied, 'You have already gained sufficient mastery of the scriptures for your age. Isn't it time for you to get settled in the next stage of life? Ask me for something else.'

Bharadvaja said, 'If you are pleased with my penance, please grant me another lifespan so that I can devote myself to the study of the Vedas.'

Indra said, 'So be it,' and vanished. Bharadvaja immersed himself again in the study of the scriptures.

Towards the end of the second 100 years, Bharadvaja realized that he hadn't completed his study and so prayed again to Indra. Once again, Indra appeared before him and granted him on request another 100 years, which he promptly spent in study. At the end of the third lifespan, he prayed to Indra again and Indra appeared before him. Bharadvaja greeted him with folded hands and prayed for one more lifespan so that he could complete his study.

Indra said, 'Great Sage, you have spent 300 years in Vedic studies observing celibacy and austerity. Don't you want anything else—fame, wealth, power? I am the king of Devas, I can grant you anything you ask.'

Bharadvaja replied unhesitatingly, 'I want to gain mastery of the scriptures. Please extend my life again so that I can achieve my goal.'

Indra smiled and said, 'You have asked for the same boon every time. Let me show you something. You want to become the master of the Vedas, right?' With a swish of his hand Indra caused three mountains of sand to appear. Pointing at them he said, 'Look at these mountains. They symbolize the knowledge contained in the Rigveda, the Yajurveda and the Samaveda. These are the mountains of knowledge you are attempting to scale'. Indra then took three fistful of sand and poured it. He continued: 'In each of your three lifespans, you have studied one fistful of Veda. What you see as these mountains represent what remains unknown to you still. The Vedas are infinite repositories of esoteric knowledge. What a human needs to lead a life of purpose is only a fistful. O Bharadvaja, take my advice and give up this endless pursuit of Vedic study. It is impossible for mortals to acquire complete knowledge of the Vedas. Put an end to these futile efforts. Use your knowledge to achieve the supreme goal of human life and impart it to your fellowmen too.'

Sage Bharadvaja prostrated to the king of Devas and thanked him. Indra blessed him and imparted to him the knowledge of *saavitraagnividyaa* (a fire ritual) by which he instantly attained the knowledge of Parabrahman. He also regained the physical state of a young lad. He then returned to the Maruts, once again a young lad but now with a vision for the future.

BHARADVAJA: ADOPTION BY BHARATA, KING OF KASI

Bharata was the son of the famed Dusyanta and the beautiful Sakuntalaa. He was ancestor to the Pandavas of the Dvaparayuga. Dusyanta was the son of Ila of the Candravamsa.

Bharata became king of Kasi by marrying Sunanda, the daughter of Sarvasena. Sunanda was virtuous and devoted to her husband. Years passed but Sunanda was unable to bear children and, much against his wishes, Bharata was forced to marry repeatedly for progeny. Three of his wives bore him nine sons in all. However, none of his sons had qualities suitable for a king. Bharata became withdrawn and lost interest in his kingly duties. His wives, frightened that he would abandon them, neglected their sons and the sons died early. Queen Sunanda, who had been a mute spectator to all this, tried to draw him out of his shell.

One day she suggested to him, 'My Lord! I have given everything to you all these years. May I make a request?' Bharata nodded and she continued, 'A king is not a father to just the sons and daughters that he sires. He is the father to all the subjects of his kingdom. As such, you must not neglect your responsibilities to your children. For the welfare of all, we must continue to perform sacrifices and rituals. We cannot lead cloistered lives. That would mean that we are not discharging our dharma.' She cajoled him and, finally, Bharata began to take interest in the welfare of the kingdom once again. On the advice of his ministers, the royal couple performed several sacrifices and prayers for begetting children.

It was when they performed the *Marutstoma* (prayers to the Maruts) that the Maruts, pleased with their offerings, appeared before them and blessed them. When asked by them what he wished for, King Bharata blurted out, 'A son is what we crave for. Please bless us with a child.' The Maruts immediately presented a lad to him and said, 'King Bharata, we are pleased with your devotion. However, we do not have the power to grant progeny. This lad has arisen from the lineage of Sage Angirasa. We have nurtured him since he was cast away by his parents. He has not known the love of a mother. You may adopt him as your own and bring him up whereby you will become parents to an illustrious child'. Sunanda kneeled and, taking the boy's hand in hers, gazed at his face, tears flowing down her cheeks. Bharata fell at the feet of the Maruts and gratefully accepted him. The adoption rituals were performed with much fanfare and gaiety. Bharata and Sunanda named the boy as Vitaha. Since he was taken by Bharata as his son, he came to be known as Bharadvaja.

Vitaha brought joy into the couple's life. Not a single day passed without Bharata and Sunanda expressing their gratitude to the Maruts for brightening up their life. Since he was already very knowledgeable, Vitaha began assisting his father in the responsibilities of administering the kingdom. Vitaha was not only just, he was compassionate towards all. When he came of age, Bharata and Sunanda called him to their chambers one evening. Sunanda seated Vitaha beside her and addressed him, 'Vitaha my son, from the day you entered our lives, our days have been full of joy. You have indeed made our life complete with your love and affection. It is the good karma of our previous lives that we have an offspring like you. Like all parents, we too would like to play with grandchildren. Your father and I feel that Princess Suseela would be a suitable companion to you. If you are willing, we shall accept her hand which has been offered by her father.'

Vitaha nodded, 'Mother, whatever you and father decide is acceptable to me.'

Years passed in family bliss and royal duties. But then Vitaha began to feel restless. He had not forgotten his stay with the Maruts or his rigorous penance to learn the Vedas, and he wanted to return to pursue that path of learning. He knew Bharata and Sunanda would never agree to his giving up kingship and leaving the palace. Vitaha was aware that his father was in fact waiting for the day when he would take over his responsibilities completely so that he and Sunanda could enter *vaanaprasthaasrama*—third stage of life in the Aryan society.

Vitaha was in the garden ruminating over his strange situation when Bharata came to him and said, 'Vitaha, you seem to be preoccupied with something of late. What is it that worries you? Will you not tell me? Maybe I can solve it in a second.'

Vitaha smiled and said, 'Father, you alone can help me. I know this will upset you and mother. You are aware of my lineage and it would not become of me to indulge in kingly pursuits instead of treading the path of spiritual learning and teaching. However, being your son, I cannot forsake my duties to the kingdom. Father, I request you, please perform a sacrifice for an offspring. I will officiate as priest. I am sure you will be blessed with another child.'

Seeing his father's panic, he continued, 'I will not abandon you if nothing comes out of the ritual. I am aware of your yearning for children before I came into your life. Please indulge me one more time. Only you can convince mother. Please Father, for my sake.'

Bharata had no choice but to resign himself to his fate and cajole Sunanda. They performed a sacrifice under the auspices of Vitaha himself. He used the spiritual wealth he had amassed to obtain a son for his parents. The son born of the sacrifice was named Bhaumanya. King Bharata and Sunanda embraced Vitaha by turn and said with emotion, 'Vitaha, you will always remain our first son.'

Vitaha, however, had to wait for many more years to leave the palace and pursue his quest for knowledge. This was because King Bharata did not live long after Bhaumanya was born. As a result, Vitaha had to stay in the palace till Bhaumanya grew old enough to be crowned king. Vitaha had to play the role of father to Bhaumanya and prepare him for his royal responsibilities.

BHARADVAJA: FROM SEEKER TO SEER

Bharadvaja's thirst for knowledge never waned throughout his life. Neither was he enamoured by the luxurious life in the palace of King Bharata, nor was he corrupted by the power of kingship. He remained a true scholar, always in search of new learnings. Once he had ensured that his brother Bhaumanya would take the kingdom to new heights, he knew it was time for him to return to his true calling.

He went to Queen Sunanda and said that he wanted to talk to her about his future. She seated him beside her and he began, 'Mother, I know that what I will now request of you will hurt you but I am sure you would always want your son to be happy. I shall forever cherish the time that I have spent with you and father. I had expressed a desire earlier to move to the forest and have my own hermitage. Now I feel it is time that I do so. Bhaumanya has grown up and is ready for kingship; I have imparted *rajadharma* (kingly duties) to him. I want you to bid me farewell with a smile and bless me and my family.' Sunanda took his hands in hers and acquiesced with a bowed head. She did not want him to see her tears. He prostrated at her feet and left her chamber without a backward glance.

The next day, Bharadvaja, his wife Suseela and his daughters, dressed in ordinary clothes, left the palace on foot with minimum belongings. Bharadvaja built a small hermitage in Prayaga, the confluence of Ganga, Yamuna and Sarasvati. He began his studies with renewed interest and vigour. Based on his life with King Bharata, he contributed to the fields of *Dharmasastra* (science of good conduct) and *Rajyasastra* (science of polity). He was quoted later by Kautilya, author of *Arthasastra*. He wrote about Sanskrit *vyaakarana* (grammar) and *sikshaa* (phonetics), and his text on them is one of the oldest, if not the oldest, though not as comprehensive as Panini's. He also contributed to the fields of *Vaastusastra* (science of dwelling-place) and *Kalpasutras* (rules on ritual), and Sutras on *srauta* (scriptural), *grhya* (domestic) and *pitrimedha* (sacrifice to pitrdevatas). He also wrote detailed treatises on Vedic rituals and culture.

Bharadvaja's fame as a person who had spent 300 years in learning the Vedas spread in all directions, and one day while meditating, he was approached by a group of sages headed by Bhrigu, who addressed him thus, 'Great Sage, the time has come for you to share the wisdom that you have amassed. All of us here would like to hear from you about the practice of *nitya* (daily obligatory) and *naimittika* (incidental obligatory) karmas. Please enlighten us.'

Bharadvaja saw Bhrigu, Angirasa, Atri, Vasishtha, Sandilya, Markandeya, Mandavya and others standing before him with folded hands. He was overwhelmed and welcomed them with open arms. Bharadvaja, who loved teaching and sharing insights, took this opportunity to produce Bharadvajasmriti (law book) for the use of all till time immemorial.

One evening, while he was watching the sunset, Suseela approached him and said, 'I see you have immersed yourself totally in your scholarly pursuits—writing, reading and teaching—but this knowledge must reach all. The common man remains enmeshed in samsara. Is there no relief for him?'

These words by Suseela pained Bharadvaja. When he met other sages in the Himalayas, he voiced his concern. All were in agreement and they realized that people are essentially good, but there are many reasons that make them stray from the path of dharma. One of the main difficulties that they face is the various diseases that plague them, for which they have no medicine. They die early; endure ill-health, which makes them unable to discharge their duties, and spend their energies in endless ailments. People need good health if they are to follow the *purushaarthas*—principal objects of human existence. What meaning will dharma, artha, kaama and moksha—right conduct, money, desire and salvation—hold for them if they are preoccupied with ill-health and hunger? How will such people aspire for knowledge, especially spiritual knowledge?

The sages felt that Indra, the king of Devas, should be approached for guidance, but none volunteered to do the same. Bharadvaja took the lead, saying, 'I will meet Indra. I have prayed to him earlier and feel that he would be able to give us a solution. I will seek him out and bring this situation to his notice.' Bharadvaja set out immediately and reached Indra's abode in no time through his spiritual powers.

He bowed to Indra and stood with folded hands like a diligent pupil. Indra was genuinely pleased to see him. 'I welcome you, Rishi Bharadvaja. I believe everything is well with you and your family. You have authored several treatises and have become well known for the erudition that you have achieved. Could it be that you seek to further your studies?' Indra asked Bharadvaja, his eyes twinkling.

Bharadvaja said, 'Devendra, you know what occurs in the remotest corners of the world. I desire to spread the Vedic knowledge to people so that they can live in dharma. I want the well-being of all, especially spiritual well-being. I see that mankind is beset with suffering from various diseases. As a representative of all those who seek to uplift mankind, I appeal to you to provide us a remedy for this situation. Please do not disappoint us.'

Indra was pleased with Bharadvaja's sense of involvement and care for the troubled. He replied, 'Rishi Bharadvaja! You have reminded me of my duty towards mankind. Many aeons ago, Lord Brahma handed over the science of medicine to his son Dakshaprajapati for dissemination to worldly beings. The latter instructed the Ashvini twins, who shared it with me as a repository. I shall transmit that knowledge to you; you shall take it to earth and see that all are benefitted from it.'

Indra then taught Ayurveda to Bharadvaja painstakingly from the basics—the fundamental doctrine of the three *doshas* (deficiencies), namely *kapha* (phlegm), *pitta* (bile) and *vaata* (wind). He then expounded the signs for recognition and identification of various diseases and their remedies.

Bharadvaja returned after completion of his task and shared the knowledge of Ayurveda with all the sages of his time. He systematically tutored Punarvasu Atreya, who in turn groomed six disciples: Bhela, Jatukarna, Parasara, Harita, Ksarapani and Agnivesa. Of these, Agnivesa turned out to be the most promising. He codified the knowledge of Ayurveda in *Agnivesasamhitaa*, which was modified later by Caraka. In this manner, *Carakasamhitaa*, the oldest Ayurvedic text still available, along with *Susrutasamhitaa*, brought succour to millions.

BHARADVAJA: SONS AND DAUGHTERS

Sage Bharadvaja and wife Suseela had two daughters. One of them, Katyayani, married Maharshi Yagyavalkya and bore him three sons—Candrakanta, Mahamegha and Vijaya. The other daughter, Devavarnini, married Sage Visrava and had a son Vaisravana, also called Kubera, who was later appointed as the *dikpala* (regent or lord) of the north. Indra, Yama and Varuna had already been made dikpalas of the east, south and west, respectively. Kubera was also entrusted with the care of wealth.

Bharadvaja fathered many sons, one of whom was Damana, a highly evolved spiritual seeker. As soon as his father performed his upanayanam, Damana set off to the Himalayas. Near Amarakantaka, he met the hermit Garga who described to him the glories of Kasi, the eternal city of Siva. This had such an effect on Damana that he forgot his travel to the Himalayas and sat down there itself for penance. After several years of severe penance, he left his mortal body and attained heaven.

Another son of Bharadvaja was Sukesa. In his pursuit of knowledge of the Parabrahman, Sukesa went with five others to the asrama of Pippalada, son of Sage Dadhici. Pippalada welcomed them and asked them to stay with him for a year and observe celibacy, after which they would get answers for their questions. A year passed and each of them asked his question and got the answer. Sukesa's question was, 'Where does one find the *purusha* (person) of *shodasakalaas* (16 parts)?' Pippalada explained: 'Parabrahman created life. From life, faith and, then followed, space, air, light, water, earth, sense organs, mind, food. From food sprang vitality, penance, hymns, work, worlds and names. When these 16 parts tending towards the purusha disappear, their name and form are broken up, and one speaks only of the purusha. That one is what has no parts and is immortal.'

Pippalada concluded that only thus far he knew of Parabrahman and there was nothing higher than that. Sukesa and the others returned home satisfied with the answers given by Pippalada.

BHARADVAJA: GUIDING LIGHT OF THE KASI KINGS

Sage Bharadvaja's knowledge, coupled with experience in polity and administration, made him a sought-after person by kings who came to him from afar for guidance. Many of the kings appealed to him to grace their court and become their preceptor. But Bharadvaja would not be swayed to leave his hermitage.

For several 100 years, the kingdoms of Kasi and Vatsa had been under the reign of a single king who ruled from Kasi. During the time of Bharadvaja, Kasi and Vatsa became separate strongholds, both ruled by strong and valiant kings. While Haryasva was content with his Kasi, Vitahavya of Vatsa wanted to take control of Kasi and merge the two kingdoms.

Vitahavya was of the Manu dynasty and a descendent of King Saryati. Vitahavya had 10 wives and sired 100 sons. His sons grew up to be brave and mighty warriors. Vitahavya with his 100 sons invaded Kasi, swarming into the city like locusts, killing all who came in their way. Haryasva and his army fought valiantly but the battle did not last long. After the death of Haryasva, Vitahavya returned to Vatsa drunk on victory. The people of Kasi rallied around Sudeva, son of Haryasva, and crowned him king. Prince Sudeva had been away from Kasi when Haryasva was defeated. When

Vitahavya heard about Sudeva's coronation, his anger knew no bounds. He sent his 100 sons again. Though Sudeva was a valiant warrior in his own right, he had had no time to recoup his armies from the previous assault. He fought heroically but was overpowered and killed.

On hearing the news of her husband's death on the battlefield, Sudeva's wife fled the palace with her son Divodasa. Vitahavya's 100 sons returned to Vatsa with the news of their victory. Divodasa followed his father's footsteps, he returned to the palace with his mother after Vitahavya's army had left Kasi and sat on the throne. He immediately tried to fortify the city but Vitahavya and his sons returned again and attacked Kasi from all sides. Divodasa faced them bravely but their fierce assaults made him realize that he had no choice but to flee and return later with fortifications. This time, Vitahavya left some of his sons in Kasi before returning to Vatsa.

Divodasa wandered in the forests and reached the asrama of Sage Bharadvaja, who received him and his small retinue. Once Divodasa had rested, he approached Sage Bharadvaja and, falling at his feet, said, 'Please become my mentor. I have heard much about your wisdom and learning. Help me save Kasi'.

Hearing Divodasa's plea, Sage Bharadvaja asked him to narrate everything. Divodasa immediately did so. Instead of showing sympathy, Sage Bharadvaja was enraged, 'You call yourself a king, a Kshatriya! You turned your back and fled the battlefield forgetting your subjects and leaving them to face death and misery. You do not seem to be aware of rajadharma.'

Divodasa begged him to show pity and understanding. 'I fled from Kasi only for my subjects. I am no coward. I am childless and in the event of my death, to whom could I hand over Kasi? I will fight and win back my kingdom and lead it to prosperity. I need help to build my army. I need wealth for weapons and armoury. I take refuge in you. Please accept me as your pupil and guide me.'

Sage Bharadvaja's heart melted. Kasi had been his home for many years and it was the city graced by Mahadeva. Though many kings had earlier come to him for help and had left when refused, Sage Bharadvaja felt that King Divodasa was righteous and interested in safeguarding dharma, and deserved his support. The other kings who had requested him to don the role of rajaguru (royal preceptor) and mentor them had not displayed the keen desire to uphold dharma. Sage Bharadvaja propitiated Indra and, on his advice, he called upon the Asvini twins to provide King Divodasa weaponry, wealth and skills to prepare an army. Bharadvaja took on the role of rajaguru and guided the king in all aspects.

One of his first actions as rajaguru was performing of the Putrakaameshti Yajna, a Vedic sacrifice performed by one desirous of a son. King Dasaratha had performed it on the advice of Sage Rishyasringa and was blessed with four sons: Rama, Lakshmana, Bharata and Satrughna. This yajna is usually performed after the Asvamedha Yajna. With his spiritual powers, Sage Bharadvaja ensured that Divodasa fathered a warrior son, whom he named Pratardana.

Pratardana learned all the aspects of warfare under Sage

Bharadvaja's tutelage and when he was 13, he took command of the army and declared war against Vitahavya and his 100 sons in Vatsa. The 100 sons of Vitahavya were fearless fighters, but Pratardana fought fiercely and annihilated all of them. Hearing this news, Vitahavya fled from Vatsa and sought refuge in the hermitage of Sage Bhrigu. Pratardana followed him to the asrama. There, Sage Bhrigu welcomed him, saying, 'Son Pratardana, why are you here with your army, whom are you seeking in this house of learning?'

Pratardana respectfully bowed and said: 'Sage Bhrigu! I am the son of Divodasa, King of Kasi, my name is Pratardana. The people of Kasi have suffered much at the hands of King Vitahavya of Vatsa who attacked Kasi several times to take over its kingship. You are aware of all that has happened and the death of innocents these attacks have caused. My great-grandfather and grandfather were killed mercilessly and my father has been wandering in the forests for several years facing great hardships. Under the guidance of Sage Bharadvaja, I have fought and killed the 100 sons of Vitahavya. I am now seeking to end Vitahavya's life so that I can avenge the deaths of my great-grandfather and grandfather. I have been following him since he fled the battleground. If he is hiding here, please call him out to face and fight me.'

Sage Bhrigu had given *abhaya* (assurance of safety) to King Vitahavya and, hence, he could not let him be killed. Therefore, he replied thus, 'Pratardana, there are no Kshatriyas in this hermitage. Here, all are my students and they are engaged in learning the sacred lore. You may return to your kingdom and live in peace.'

Pratardana responded, 'Sage Bhrigu, I thank you for your blessings and shall return home. If my foe has left rajadharma and taken up the study of the Vedas, I know that I have vanquished the Kshatriya in him and I will not kill a man of learning. '

After Pratardana had left with his army, Vitahavya came out of hiding and fell at Sage Bhrigu's feet. He said, 'I do not know how to thank you for saving my life. Please accept me as your disciple and allow me to live in your hermitage. I would like to spend the rest of my life in scholarship and acquiring merit. It would be a dishonour to you if I return to fight Pratardana and make your words untrue.' By the *anugraha* (grace) of Sage Bhrigu, Vitahavya, though born a Kshatriya, achieved complete mastery over the scriptures. One of his descendants by the name of Gritsamada became a seer of the highest order.

BHARADVAJA: RECLAIMING PEACE FROM DEMONIC FORCES

During the time he was in Kasi as rajaguru, Sage Bharadvaja decided to meet Sage Bhrigu who was at Mount Kailasa at that time. It was an arduous journey and, while returning, Sage Bharadvaja saw people being harassed by evil demons. Prominent among these demonic forces were the Vaarasikas and Sambara. They took great pleasure in tormenting the weak, especially those who opposed them. The Vaarasikas were a 100 in number and the eldest, Parama, with his best friend Sambara, led them in their atrocities. These demons lived on the banks of the Hariyopiya River and had mastered a technique of protecting themselves from arrows by the use of invisible armours.

Sage Bharadvaja approached Parama and advised him, 'You should desist from this kind of living as it leads to self-destruction.' Parama laughed derisively, 'Brothers, look who has come to teach us! The Great Bharadvaja! Did you know he studied for 300 years? Finally, Indra had to stop him!' Everyone joined him laughing derisively. 'Do you know our might? If you can face us, do so. Otherwise don't waste our time talking. Go away before I kill you.' As Sage Bharadvaja made his way home, he felt that he must help the victims he had seen on his path.

On reaching his hermitage, Sage Bharadvaja found King Divodasa of Kasi and his friend King Abhyavarti, son of Chayamanana, waiting. Sage Bharadvaja related his experience during his visit to Mount Kailasa. King Abhyavarti folded his hands and said, 'Sage Bharadvaja, the Vaarasikas have attacked and looted my kingdom. The demons showed no pity on the hapless women and children. King Divodasa of Kasi rushed to my assistance but we were no match for them. We seek your refuge; please shower your grace on us.' Since the odds were against them, both kings with their meagre armies had retreated into the forests and sought refuge in the hermitage of Sage Bharadvaja.

Seeing them and hearing about what had occurred, Sage

Bharadvaja was incensed. He said, 'You call yourself kings and here you are hiding, afraid for your lives. What about your people? Why have you deserted them like orphans? Fight the demons instead of fleeing like cowards. You are bringing disgrace by your diffidence.'

Abhyavarti waited till the wrath of Sage Bharadvaja subsided and then beseeched for help. 'I am no coward,' he said. 'You know me well. I am ready to sacrifice myself for the safety of my people. If I have come here, it is only to plead for my people. My soldiers are not armed, clothed or fed. How can I descend into the battlefield and send them to certain death? Would that be rajadharma? Please bless me in obtaining the support of the gods, so that these demons can be vanquished.'

Bharadvaja was appeased with the king's words. He immediately invoked Lord Indra, who provided wealth and weapons for the army.

King Abhyavarti confidently went to the battlefield. After a long drawn-out confrontation, he finally managed to decimate all the Vaarasikas, including Parama, and freed his people. Hearing the news of his friend's death, Shambara ransacked Kasi in the absence of King Divodasa. King Divodasa and Abhyavarti joined forces and with the guidance and blessings of Sage Bharadvaja, fought Shambara. In the fierce struggle that ensued, Divodasa invoked Indra and, instilling the power given to him in an arrow, cut off Shambara's head. Thus, righteousness was restored once again.

BHARADVAJA: GUIDE TO SRI RAMA AND BHARATA

In the Tretayuga, Lord Vishnu was born as Sri Rama in order to kill the demons Ravana and Kumbhakarna. In order to fulfil this, Queen Kaikeyi sought the banishment of Sri Rama to the forest for 14 years as a boon from Dasaratha, king of Ayodhya. Thereafter, as per King Dasaratha's boon to the queen, Sri Rama left the kingdom. He was followed by his wife Sita and his brother Lakshmana.

When Bharadvaja heard the news of Sri Rama's banishment, he was initially filled with grief and sorrow. By the insight gained from his tapas, he divined that Sri Rama would stop by his place to seek his blessings, and so he began to wait for him expectantly; he knew that Sri Rama was Lord Vishnu himself.

Sri Rama, Sita and Lakshmana reached Sage Bharadvaja's asrama at dusk when the night agnihotra was being performed. Seeing them arrive, Sage Bharadvaja joyously welcomed them. With tears in his eyes, he blessed them as they touched his feet reverentially. He said, 'Sri Rama! It would be our great fortune if you stay here in my abode for this period of exile. Please consider this as your home and grace it. There will be no restrictions on any of you during your stay here.'

Sri Rama smiled benevolently and said: 'Respected Sir! I understand your feelings and it would indeed have been a welcome suggestion. However, the proximity of this place to Ayodhya would make it impossible for me to accept your invitation. You are well aware that all the people of Ayodhya

Bharadvaja

are against my exile and will definitely come here repeatedly to persuade me to return if I choose to stay here. This will create an impediment to your rituals and penance. We must go far away to avoid all this. Kindly excuse my refusal of your heartfelt invitation.'

Sri Rama then continued, 'We would actually need your advice as to the direction and distance we must cover before we can settle down. We would be happy if you can indicate a suitable route and place for stay since you are knowledgeable of the terrain of this forested area.'

Sage Bharadvaja smilingly replied, 'In my opinion, Citrakuta would be the ideal place for your purpose. In Citrakuta, animals, especially bears and monkeys, roam freely. Citrakuta abounds in fruits, roots and honey and is most suited for dwelling in these forests. Many sages have sanctified the area by living there till they attained heaven. I can help you with the directions in the morning. Please stay here for tonight and sanctify all of us with your presence.' Sage Bharadvaja then made arrangements for their stay and Suseela herself prepared the night's meal.

The next morning, at the crack of dawn, Sage Bharadvaja woke up and made necessary arrangements for performing the *svastyayana* ceremony—the ceremony of averting evil by recitation of mantras. It was a custom to perform this ritual before proceeding on a journey for attaining prosperity. He then advised them on the path to Citrakuta and told them how to reach the huge banyan tree there. He then bade farewell to them with his blessings, 'May your journey be auspicious'.

A few days had passed when Sri Rama's younger brother Bharata arrived at Sage Bharadvaja's asrama, accompanied by a horde of Ayodhya residents. Kulaguru Vasishtha, brother Satrughna, advisors and ministers were also part of the group. Sage Bharadvaja accorded all of them a royal welcome, 'Please come in to my humble abode, Prince Bharata, Sage Vasishtha, Prince Satrughna and others. I am honoured by your arrival.' He then tried to console Prince Bharata: 'I am aware of all that has happened in Ayodhya. I know you are distressed with the events but you must realize that not even a blade of grass moves without the will of Parabrahman. The future is destined and must be taken in one's stride. Do not hold yourself or your mother responsible for any of the happenings or their aftermath. Treat your mother with reverence and kindness. She was just an instrument in this play of the universe. I am aware as to why you are here but would like to hear from you the reasons for the same.'

Bharata replied sorrowfully, 'O Great Sage! What other reason can I have other than seeking to take my brother Sri Rama home? My mother's selfish demand has caused my father's death and the 14 years exile of my dearest brother who is the rightful heir to the throne. I am here to undo the wrongdoings of my mother in my absence. I will somehow persuade my brother to return and accept the crown that is rightfuly his. I am only his slave and wish to serve him. Please tell me how to reach my brother, I beg of you.'

Sage Bharadvaja, pleased with Bharata's words said, 'You

are righteous and devoted to Sri Rama. So I shall describe the path that will lead you to him in the morning. Please spend the night here in my hermitage. I would be honoured if you consume food with me.' Prince Bharata reluctantly agreed remembering his huge retinue and wondering if Sage Bharadvaja knew about it. Sage Bharadvaja left, smiling to himself at the awkwardness of Prince Bharata.

By the power of his tapas, he summoned Visvakarma, the architect of Devas, and got a magnificent hall constructed. He called upon Gandharvas to wait upon and serve all. Bharata was stunned at the arrangements and the lavish spread that was placed in front of him and his entourage. The next morning, Sage Bharadvaja bid adieu to Prince Bharata after having directed him on the path to Citrakuta.

Prince Bharata reached Citrakuta but was unable to convince Sri Rama to return to Ayodhya. Sri Rama was firm about completing the exile period of 14 years. Bharata, therefore, requested his brother to give his *paadukas* (footwear) to him so that Ayodhya could be ruled on Sri Rama's behalf by Bharata, with the placement of the paadukas on the throne. Bharata further took a vow that if Sri Rama did not return immediately after the completion of the exile period, he would consign his body to fire. On his way back, Prince Bharata stopped again at Sage Bharadvaja's hermitage and narrated in detail all that occurred in his meeting with his brother. Sage Bharadvaja was impressed with Bharata's devotion and steadfastness and blessed him.

Fourteen years later, Sage Bharadvaja received the

returning Sri Rama, Sita and Lakshmana and, on his request, Sri Rama again stayed the night at his hermitage. Sage Bharadvaja revealed that he had been aware of all the future events when he had met Sri Rama the first time and related all that had happened in Ayodhya during Sri Rama's exile. Overwhelmed by happiness at Sri Rama's homecoming, Sage Bharadvaja offered to grant him a boon but Sri Rama refused. Sage Bharadvaja insisted and Sri Rama finally accepted a boon from him: he requested that his kingdom of Saaketa be always surrounded by greenery, flowers and fruits till a distance of hundred yojanas (one yojana is 14.48 kilometres). Sage Bharadvaja demonstrated once again that he possessed all qualities needed for a sage in addition to the power earned by his tapas

BHARADVAJA AND RAIBHYA: TEST OF FRIENDSHIP

Sage Bharadvaja and Sage Raibhya were the greatest of friends. Bharadvaja's son Yavakrita lived with him. Raibhya had two sons, Paravasu and Aravasu, both equally learned in the scriptures and the performance of sacrificial rites. Though Bharadvaja and Raibhya were highly learned, it was Raibhya and his sons who were revered by the people. Bharadvaja was a true ascetic, involved in the pursuit of *aatmajnaana* (knowledge of Self), and he cared not for people's adulation. But Yavakrita was envious of Raibhya and his sons, and decided to do something about it.

Yavakrita was indolent, and Bharadvaja's many attempts

to teach him failed. Yavakrita decided to perform penance to Indra for attaining knowledge. He approached his father to take his permission. Bharadvaja advised him, 'My son, the acquisition of knowledge requires effort and perseverance, not penance. Instead of doing tapas, why don't you seek a guru?'

Yavakrita replied, 'Father, you have mentioned many times that you are very dear to Indra. Indra is the most benevolent of the Devas. I am determined to please him and gain the boon of knowledge. I want to excel against Sage Raibhya's sons.'

'Dearest boy,' Sage Bharadvaja said, 'Your desire to acquire jnaana is not only appropriate for a rishiputra but also highly commendable. But the path you have chosen is not proper. And this envy of yours will only destroy you, don't allow it any place in your heart, it will consume you and reduce you to ashes.' But Yavakrita was adamant and Sage Bharadvaja had to agree.

Yavakrita's rigorous penance compelled Indra to appear. 'Tell me, Yavakrita, son of Bharadvaja, why have you called me? Are you desirous of wealth and prosperity? Cattle and kingdoms? Women? Whatever you want I shall grant.'

'No Lord Indra, King of the Devas, it is knowledge I seek. Bless me that the Vedas dance on my fingertips so that kings and emperors seek me, the people revere me and the sages adore me.'

'Yavakrita, you are the son of my dear Bharadvaja, he who devoted three lifespans to the study of the Vedas. Only to gain a fistful! I never expected such a request from you, you disappoint me. Ask something else,' Indra said.

'No, I do not want anything else,' Yavakrita answered. 'Well then,' and Indra disappeared.

Yavakrita narrated the entire incident to his father. Bharadvaja gave a sad smile but made no reply. The next day Yavakrita went to the river for his bath. There, he saw an old man sitting on the bank and throwing fistfuls of sand into the water. Finding the scene absurd, Yavakrita asked the old man what he was doing. The old man replied, 'I am building a bridge,' and continued with his task.

Yavakrita burst into laughter. 'Building a bridge! Are you out of your mind? Can't you see it is impossible to build a bridge with handfuls of sand?'

The old man coolly replied, 'Not as impossible as your wish to obtain knowledge without effort.'

Yavakrita stopped laughing, 'You must be Lord Indra. Do you mean to say that it is impossible for the king of Devas to grant me this wish?'

Indra sighed in exasperation and said tersely, 'If you refuse to see reason, even the gods cannot help you. Your wish is granted.' And he vanished.

Yavakrita was thrilled and rushed to his father to inform him. Sage Bharadvaja was agitated and warned his son to guard himself against pride. He said, 'If you gain knowledge without effort you shall not value it. Do not allow your head to become swollen. And do not go near Sage Raibhya's asrama, that's an order.'

Yavakrita's fame spread like wildfire; he was honoured by kings and sought by scholars. Despite his father's advice, one day, he went to Sage Raibhya's asrama. The sage and his two sons were away. Only his daughter-in-law, Paravasu's wife, was at home. He forcibly entered the asrama despite her protests and molested her.

When Sage Raibhya returned and found his daughter-in-law in tears, he divined what had happened to her. Mad with rage, he pronounced an incantation, and from the sacrificial fire arose a demon. Sage Raibhya ordered the demon to kill Yavakrita. The demon chased Yavakrita right up to his father's hermitage and slew him at the entrance.

The sight of his son's slaughter in front of his eyes and his own helplessness broke Sage Bharadvaja's heart. He knew that his son's misdeed was deserving of death, yet his love for his son took primacy over his emotions. In his grief, Sage Bharadvaja cursed his friend Sage Raibhya, 'You have caused me untold grief by killing my son. You too shall die. And you shall die at the hands of your own son.' The next moment Sage Bharadvaja was overcome by remorse. But he could not retract his curse. He decided that he did not want to live any longer. He performed the last rites of his son and threw himself into the same funeral pyre. However, his curse did come true.

One evening, Sage Raibhya was walking in front of his hermitage waiting for his sons to return. He had covered himself with a deerskin as it was very cold. Approaching in the darkness of dusk, his elder son Paravasu mistook him for an animal and killed him.

Paravasu went to the king and complained that his

younger brother was responsible for their father's death and had him ostracized. Aravasu left the kingdom and prayed to Siva with such intensity that he appeared before him and asked him his desire.

Aravasu said, 'You are aware of all that has happened. I want my father alive and his good friend Sage Bharadvaja with him. Though Bharadvaja's son committed a sin, he has been punished for it, so please restore his life also. In this manner I will be freed of the accusations that have been heaped on me and my brother Paravasu will accept me back. Please grant the happiness and contentment that was ours.'

The munificent Siva was pleased with Aravasu: he had asked nothing for himself. Siva granted his wishes and disappeared. Raibhya, Bharadvaja and Yavakrita came into being again. Yavakrita fell at the feet of Sage Raibhya and asked for forgiveness. He then begged his father to overlook his folly in not heeding his advice. Sage Raibhya and Sage Bharadvaja looked at each other with eyes filled with tears of mixed emotions—happiness and remorse.

Later, Paravasu returned to the king and told him all that had happened and begged forgiveness for his actions. The king in turn invited Aravasu and sought his pardon.

BHARADVAJA: PIONEER OF AVIATION AND AERIAL WEAPONRY

In addition to Vedic knowledge, Sage Bharadvaja evinced interest in science and technology. He was particularly interested in mechanical, aerospace and aeronautical engineering.

In the Krita or Satyayuga, people attained *ashtasiddhis* (eight accomplishments) by practising certain austerities. This enabled them to move things as well as move from place to place. In the Tretayuga, vehicles had been designed which could be flown by the chanting of hymns or mantras. Pushpaka Vimana used by Ravana was one such vehicle. In the Dvaparayuga, *tantras* (rituals) were used to fly vehicles. In the Kaliyuga, people have no inherent or learned skills to make anything move or to move from one place to another. They have to depend on mechanical or electronic machines.

Sage Bharadvaja's treatise *Yantrasarvasva*, also known as *Brihadvimanasastra*, has encompassing details of aviation, space science and flying machines. These writings of Sage Bharadvaja were the inspiration for several related theses and expositions. Saunaka wrote *Vyomayaanatantra*, Garga wrote *Yantrakalpa*, Vachaspati essayed *Yaanabindu*, Caakraayani wrote *Khetayaanapradeepikaa*, Dundi Natha wrote the *Vyomayaanaarkaprakaasa* and Yantra Lalla wrote *Kalpataru*.

Sage Bharadvaja designed flying machines that could fly not only from one place to another on earth but also from one loka to another (from one planet to another) and from one universe to another. By the application of solar, wind and electrical forces, these flying machines could be made visible or invisible. He elaborated that one could also see incidents and hear conversations that were happening elsewhere in the world without being physically present there.

Sage Bharadvaja discussed the 32 techniques to fly a *vimana* (aircraft). In fact, many of the weaponry and missiles used during the war between Sri Rama and Ravana as well as in the great war in the Mahabharata show how the techniques advocated by Sage Bharadvaja were put to use. Thus, his brilliant inventions rightly entitle him to be called one of the earliest pioneers of aviation and space technology.

BHARADVAJA AND GHRITAACII

It was during one of Sage Bharadvaja's penances when he was away from his family that he fathered Drona. One day, as was his daily practice, he was going to the Ganga for his morning rituals. As he neared the banks of the river, a beautiful woman emerged out of the water. He observed that the sari she was wearing enhanced the loveliness of her frame. When she saw him, she shyly turned her head away and vanished from the place. She was Ghritaacii, an apsaraa from Indra's court. Sage Bharadvaja had his mind in control but his bodily reaction overtook him. He collected the semen from his ejaculation in a *drona* (wooden vessel). From it, a child emerged. Hence, Sage Bharadvaja named the baby Drona and took him home.

Bharadvaja taught Drona everything—from the Vedas and philosophy to the art of warfare and archery. Drona continued his study of the usage of various weapons under a student of Bharadvaja called Agnivesa. Drona later taught the Kuru princes—the Pandavas and Kauravas—and also played a very decisive role in the Mahabharata war. Obeying his father, Drona married Kripi, the daughter of Sage Saradvanta, son of Sage Gotama.

When Bharadvaja chanced upon the heavenly Ghritaacii on another occasion, he had the same reaction to her loveliness. This time, a daughter, Srutavati, was born. When she came of age, she desired to obtain Indra as her husband. Sage Bharadvaja tried his utmost to dissuade her but she was adamant and engaged in rigorous penance. Indra decided to test her and approached her in the guise of Sage Vasishtha. Srutavati welcomed him and Indra gave her five fruits and asked her to cook them for him. Despite using all the firewood available, Srutavati found that the fruits were not cooked, so she cut off her limbs and used them as fuel. When she presented the cooked fruits, Indra was immensely pleased and appeared in his true form. He restored her limbs and accepted her as his wife with Sage Bharadvaja's blessings.

7

Gotama

yogaadhyah sarvabhuutaanaam annadaanaratassadaa |
ahalyaayaahpatih sriimaan gotamah sarvapaavanah ||*

Rich in yogic practice, one who gives food to all creatures, husband of pious Ahalya, respectable for all is Gotama.

GOTAMA: SAGE PAR EXCELLENCE

Sage Gotama is one of the mantradrashtaarah and, though not a maanasaputra of Lord Brahma, became part of the saptarshis of the present manvantara. He was the son of Dirghatamas and his wife Pradveshini. Dirghatamas was born blind and, hence,

---

*Visvanatha, *Vratacuudaamani*, Vaavilla Ramaswamy Sastrulu and Sons, Chennai, 1935.

was named so. However, he regained his sight by pleasing Agni through his hymns. Both Dirghatamas and Sage Bharadvaja belong to the line of Sage Angirasa. Dirghatamas studied the scriptures from his father Sage Utathya who propounded the truth of *ekam sat* (only One exists). Gotama, being the son of Dirghatamas, was thus Sage Bharadvaja's nephew. The moment Gotama was born, the surrounding darkness was scattered due to the radiance emanating from the child and the entire area was lit up. Hence, he was named Gotama (go meaning light, tamas meaning darkness).

Sage Gotama authored many hymns in the first mandala of the Rigveda. A hymn called 'Bhadra' in the Samaveda is also ascribed to Sage Gotama. Of his two sons, Vamadeva and Nodhas, Vamadeva is attributed to have written the fourth book of the Rigveda. Sage Gotama expounded the Nyayasutras, logic and reasoning (based on his conversations with Lord Dharma); Gautamasamhitaa, an astrological text, and the Pitrmedhasutra (aphorisms on sacrifices to the manes). His Dharmasutras, known as Gautamasutras, consists of 28 chapters with about a 1,000 aphorisms and covers all aspects of the Sanatana Dharma. Some of the topics covered in this work are the varna system, the four asramas, the 40 samskaras, duties of a king, crime and punishment, funeral rites to be observed, rules of atonement, dharma for women, food and rules for food consumption, property, inheritance and so on.

Even before King Bhagiratha became famous for bringing Gangaa to earth, Sage Gotama had pleased Lord Siva, in whose locks Goddess Gangaa resides, and as a result, both came down to dwell on earth—Lord Siva as Tryambakeshvara and Gangaa as Godavari or Gautami near Brahmagiri Mountains. Later, after Bhagiratha brought Gangaa to earth, Godavari or Gautami began to be referred to as Vriddhagangaa.

Gotama married Ahalya (one of impeccable beauty), a woman who lacked nothing. Ahalya was an ayonijaa as she was a maanasaputri of Lord Brahma. Ahalya became the first of the *pancaka* (group of five) whose names, when uttered, remove the sins of the person who chants them.

Sataananda, the son of Ahalya and Sage Gotama, became the *purohita* (chief priest) of King Janaka of Mithila. Shatananda was the chief priest when Sita and Sri Rama got married. Shatananda expressed his gratitude to Sri Rama for having restored his mother Ahalya to her original form from a rock. Gotama's other sons were Sharadvanta and Cirakari. Sharadvanta fathered the famous warrior Kripa as well as his sister Kripi, who became the wife of Drona. Some of Gotama's disciples were Praachinayogya, Shandilya and Gargya. Gotama and Ahalya also adopted Sugreeva and Vali, sons born to Aruna (Vinata's half-formed child and charioteer of Sun God) through Surya and Indra.

GOTAMA WEDS AHALYA

When the Kshiirasaagara (milky ocean) was churned by Devas and Asuras, many precious things were obtained. At the end, amrita was handed to them by Dhanvantari and both the groups wanted to take it for themselves. Then Vishnu took the form of Mohini, a beautiful damsel, and said that she would distribute it evenly among the Devas and Asuras. When they saw her beauty, everyone felt that none of Lord Brahma's beautiful creations was in any way equal to the beauty of Mohini. It escalated to a point where everyone believed that Lord Brahma was incapable of beautiful creation as he has become very old. This hurt Lord Brahma's pride when he heard it; he took it as a challenge. He meditated, and from the power of his penance created a girl—a perfect manifestation of beauty—exceeding the beauty of even Mohini. He named her Ahalya as she was faultless and had no blemishes. She was born of Lord Brahma's mind and hence became his first maanasaputri. The baby was so beautiful that Lord Brahma was worried about her upbringing. He, therefore, summoned Sage Gotama to his presence.

When Sage Gotama prostrated to Lord Brahma and stood dutifully to know why he had been called, he was taken aback when Lord Brahma handed over a wee child to him and instructed him thus, 'Gotama, you have pleased Mahadeva himself with your penance and gained mastery over the Self. You are fully versed in the scriptures, not just in words but also in their spirit. I would like you to bring up this baby, whom I have named Ahalya, in your hermitage along with your disciples and ensure that she receives loving care and education. Once she comes of age and attains puberty, please bring her back to me.' This was unprecedented, but Gotama knew better than to question Lord Brahma.

He returned to his hermitage in Brahmagiri and brought up the child as per instructions. When she was five years old, Ahalya began her studies with the other pupils and quickly gained knowledge of all the Sastras. Though Ahalya was the most beautiful of all women created by Lord Brahma, Sage Gotama never noticed her enchanting beauty—such was his steadfastness. Her intelligence and dedication prompted him to take her assistance in compiling the Dharmasutras. He intended it to be a comprehensive tome and cover all aspects of Sanatana Dharma.

When Ahalya came of age, Gotama promptly took her back to Lord Brahma. The look on Lord Brahma's face sufficed for Gotama—the responsibility that had been entrusted to him had been well discharged. Lord Brahma smiled at him, 'Gotama, I am extremely pleased with you. You may be aware that there were many who questioned my judgement of entrusting Ahalya to your care, but you have proved me right. Now she is not only the most beautiful woman in the world, she is also the most accomplished.' Lord Brahma turned to the Devas who were present and continued, 'I intend to arrange a competition and I want all present here to participate in it. The winner will receive Ahalya's hand in marriage.' Gotama opened his mouth to protest but decided not to. However, he noticed the astonishment on the face of the others. It was no secret that the king of Devas, Indra, desired Ahalya.

Many Devas, Yakshas, Gandharvas and even a few sages, including Gotama, participated in the contest. Lord Brahma announced that whosoever circled the earth in the shortest time would be the winner. As Gotama started off, he came across the heavenly cow Kaamadhenu giving birth to a calf. Seeing her, Gotama prostrated to the cow and went around Kaamadhenu and her baby three times. According to the Sastras, it was equivalent to going round the earth. After that, the thoughts of the competition vanished from his mind and he returned to Brahmagiri. But soon, he received news that Lord Brahma had ordered him to appear before him. Wondering what awaited him, Gotama reached Brahmaloka.

Lord Brahma welcomed him with these words: 'Gotama, I knew that you would make the perfect spouse for my dear daughter Ahalya, but I was doubtful if you would agree. Who else would have remained unenamoured of her beauty, that too in such close proximity? It is no surprise that you are dear to Mahadeva. That is why I arranged the competition. You defeated everyone with your wisdom and resourcefulness. Circumambulation of a cow that is giving birth is equivalent to circling the earth. But the others did not even notice Kaamadhenu; so engrossed were they in this pursuit that they forgot their dharma. I know you are much older than Ahalya but you are still the winner in the competition and the rightful suitor. Come forward, Gotama, and accept the hand of Ahalya. May the two of you bring forth many sons and may the world benefit from your good deeds. My blessings are with you both.'

The couple was blessed by all who had gathered. Thus, Lord Brahma gave Ahalya's hand in marriage to Gotama, inspite of the age difference.

After Sage Gotama and Ahalya had left, Lord Brahma glanced around at the defeated suitors of Ahalya. All of them, with the exception of Indra, looked ashamed and downcast. Lord Brahma allowed his glance to linger till Indra turned his face away. Indra desired Ahalya, but when he lost her to Gotama in a competition, he was greatly dismayed and began waiting for an opportunity to win her.

Sage Gotama brought Ahalya to his asrama again. Brahmagiri, which was earlier a hermitage, now became their home.

GOTAMA CURSES AHALYA

From the day Lord Brahma married Ahalya to Gotama, Indra, who was desirous of her, was waiting for an opportunity. One day, very early in the morning, that is, before dawn, he came to the hermitage and crowed like a cock. Hearing it, Gotama thought that the day had broken and rose from the bed. As was his routine every morning, Gotama went to the Ganga for his morning bath. He glanced upwards at the sky. The stars were shining brightly. It seemed darker than usual along his path. He reached the river, placed his clothes on a nearby stone and was about to step into the water. Goddess Gangaa appeared before him and bade him not to enter. Gotama was astonished. Such an incident had never occurred before. Gangaa addressed him, 'O best of rishis, pray tell me why have you come to bathe so early? It is just past midnight.' Gotama folded his hands in salutation and replied politely,

'Mother, has the day not yet dawned? I heard the rooster crow.' Gangaa's eyes were soft and sorrowful. 'No, my son. You are mistaken,' she said.

Gotama was puzzled. He quickly collected his clothes, saluted Gangaa again and strode thoughtfully towards his hut. In the meantime, Indra had entered the hermitage disguised as Gotama. Sage Gotama was almost in the hut when he beheld a man in his guise emerging from within and sneak away. In the darkness, Gotama was not able to see the person clearly. He feared for his wife. He entered the hut and saw that Ahalya was wide awake. She looked at him in surprise. He stared at her. Slowly, realization dawned on him. His vision became blurred as tears flowed profusely. He tried to stop them—tears of anger, tears of sorrow and frustration, even of humiliation—but could not. He turned his face away, not because Ahalya would see but because he did not want to see her face. What would be the expression on her face? Triumphant, smug, guilty, frightened or remorseful? Surely she had committed the sin unknowingly. However, Gotama was in no mood to pardon her.

A similar incident that had occurred some years ago flashed across his mind. Gotama had returned from a visit to his parents. He had observed some changes in Ahalya's demeanour. Without any proof, he had suspected his wife of an indiscretion and had voiced his doubts to her openly. Ahalya had been taken aback but she had pleaded innocence. However, he had stomped off to the forests in search of a quiet place, but not before ordering his son Cirakari to kill her.

Though Sataananda and Saradvanta were also at home, it was Cirakari on whom his eyes fell first, and he thanked God for that. When his agitated mind had calmed down, he wondered if he had been hasty in his decision. Ahalya had been devoted and chaste. She was not only a dutiful wife but also a caring mother to his children. And he had condemned Ahalya to be killed by her own son. He concluded that his action of condemning her had been hasty and terribly wrong. He hoped his son Cirakari was still debating his action. Gotama had almost run home, and when Ahalya came forward to welcome him, he could not believe his good fortune.

He sought out Cirakari, who was sitting in the backyard with a sharp knife at his side, engrossed in thought. That was Cirakari: he never took any decision or committed any action till he had spent hours debating with himself. Gotama had berated the boy several times—he disliked his tardiness—but this time, he was overjoyed. He hugged him tightly and praised him for his propensity of weighing the pros and cons prior to taking any action.

This time, however, Ahalya stood mutely with her head bent, not a word passed through her lips. He wished she would say something to assuage his feelings of outrage. Was she indeed guilty? No, no, how could he even entertain such a thought! But then how could she remain unmoved? Then, the figure of the fleeing person came to mind, and he burst out like a volcano. 'You deserve to be unseen from the eyes of the world, may you be turned into a stone by the end of today!'

A thunderous roar split the air, and Ahalya's eyes widened with disbelief, her mouth agape.

She crumpled to the ground and started to cry. 'And may that lover of yours lose his testes so that he can never repeat this action,' he heard himself utter. The asrama reverberated with the words Gotama had uttered. Indra, who went back to the heavens, was not remorseful. Instead, he continued in his wayward deeds by obtaining a ram's testes in place of his own.

The asrama suddenly looked desolate. Gotama could not stay there without his dear Ahalya. He decided to go to the Himalayas for penance. As he moved towards the door, he suddenly found Ahalya holding his feet tightly. 'My Lord, please forgive me, I cannot live without you. I have done no wrong intentionally. I was not aware that he was an imposter. I was surprised that you approached me at that time of the night but how could I say no to my lord? Please revoke your curse.'

'I cannot revoke a curse once it is uttered,' Gotama said sorrowfully. 'I have to go. You know I cannot stay here anymore,' and he tried to free his feet, but Ahalya did not let go.

She kept repeating, 'Forgive me.' After some reluctant effort, Gotama freed himself and moved forward but stopped in his tracks when he heard her say, 'My Lord, how long will I suffer separation from you? Please tell me how I must atone for this sin of mine. Do not leave me and go! Who will redeem me?'

He paused and replied, 'Lord Narayana will descend on

earth as Sri Rama in the Tretaayuga. Await his visit to our hermitage.' And without looking back, he went away.

And so Ahalya was turned to stone and her penance began. After Sri Rama and Lakshmana fought Subaahu and Maariica, Sage Visvamitra led them to Gotama's deserted hermitage on their way to Mithila. When Sri Rama's foot touched the stone, Ahalya assumed human form and was redeemed of all her sins. Her husband Sage Gotama appeared then and embraced her, and they prostrated together to Sri Rama.

GOTAMA PLEASES VARUNA

After Ahalya's redemption from Gotama's curse by Sri Rama, they began to live happily once again at the base of the Brahmagiri Mountain at the south of Jambudveepa. Their married life was a model for all. The couple's happiness was, however, short-lived. One year, Brahmagiri and the surrounding regions were struck with a severe drought. The place turned from green to brown. Plants withered away and the trees became dried stumps of wood. Streams and ponds that had water aplenty became parched. People began moving away to other places in search of water. In this manner, 12 years rolled by. Gotama and Ahalya silently witnessed the sufferings of the people, cherishing the hope that the gods would eventually take pity and shower rains. When there was no sign of any relief, Sage Gotama began to perform rigorous penance to Varuna.

Sage Gotama chose to propitiate Varuna, the god of the seas, instead of Indra, the king of Devas. Sage Gotama knew that Indra was unhappy about losing Ahalya and nursed a grudge. Varuna was not only bountiful, he was also merciful. Pleased with Sage Gotama's single-minded devotion, Varuna appeared before him. 'Sage Gotama!' he said, 'What do you desire? I am here to grant you whatever you ask for.'

Gotama was ready with his reply. 'Lord Varuna, I am blessed with your appearance. I have all that I need and am happy with whatever has been given to me. But the suffering of others pains me. There has been no rain for 12 long years. Human and animal lives have reached the bounds of endurance. Have pity on them. Shower your grace on this accursed land.'

Varuna shook his head sadly and said, 'Sage Gotama, you are a jnaani. Are you not aware that we are but instruments in the hands of the Parabrahman? We cannot transcend the framework of rules and responsibilities designed by the Parabrahman. The law demands that there should be no rain in this place for a long period of time. All the pancabhuutas (five elements: earth, space, water, fire and air) are governed by the Parabrahman and I cannot go against the law.' Gotama remained silent. Varuna continued, 'Ask me something that I can grant you. I cannot return to my abode without giving you a boon.'

Gotama modified his request. 'Please bless that I have water at my disposal at all times.'

Varuna's face lighted up with a bright smile and he replied.

'Your wish will be fulfilled. Dig a pond at this place and you shall have water always. Plant this everlasting lotus in it,' and he vanished handing over a lotus to Sage Gotama.

Gotama did as he was told by Varuna. As soon as he and his disciples finished the task, the pond was filled with clear water. News of the pond and its sweet water spread in all directions. The rishis and other people who had left the place began to return with their families. The pond became the centre point around which all their daily routines and rituals revolved. More and more people came and settled down, but the water remained at the same level. The greenery returned and so did the happiness of the people. The fauna and flora flourished again and the wild cries of the birds and animals were heard. The forest became one of the densest in the area. Everyone praised Gotama.

GOTAMA BRINGS GANGAA TO EARTH

The memories of the drought and its accompanying miseries faded from the minds of people all too soon. Water was plentiful and the surroundings green. The pond created by Sage Gotama and filled by Lord Varuna was inexhaustible and satisfied the needs of all. Every morning, disciples studying in the gurukula would go to bring water from the pond for the daily rituals and other household needs. In a gurukula, all the disciples are given duties by the guru and his wife. While some would bring water, some would gather firewood, some would collect fruits and tubers for food, others would take the cattle for grazing.

One morning Gotama's disciples went to the pond as usual to collect water for the daily rituals. The wives of the other rishis were already at the pond. The disciples politely sought their consent to take water for their guru, but were told to wait for their turn. They waited for some time hoping that the women would give them a chance soon. But the ladies unconcernedly immersed themselves in their duties of washing and cleaning clothes and utensils.

After some time, the boys made their request again. This time, the rishis' wives rudely answered, 'Don't you see that we are not done yet? You have come after us, so you must wait for your turn. Don't hurry us.'

However, the disciples were immature. They retorted, 'Our guru, Sage Gotama, has created this pond and everyone should be grateful to him. We do not want him to wait for water to perform holy rituals. Do hurry up.' The women uttered vile remarks and shouted threats at them. Unable to face them, the disciples hurried back to the hermitage and reported everything to Ahalya.

Ahalya accompanied the pupils to the pond. As she approached, she could hear the women making comments but she ignored them. When she reached the pond, the women gave way in silence and the students collected water quickly. As they turned their backs to return, the silence was broken again. The women continued with their remarks and Ahalya was glad when she could hear them no more. Ahalya mentioned the incident to her husband without going into the details. She was aware that Gotama was very sensitive and did not want to hurt him. However, it was not to be so.

The wives of the other rishis not only narrated the happenings to their respective husbands but also complained that Gotama and Ahalya were nasty and hostile to them and that the couple needed to be taught a lesson. The rishis were carried away by their wives' tales. They performed penance to Ganesa, and when he appeared before them, asked him to drive away Gotama and his family from Brahmagiri. Ganesa tried his utmost to dissuade them but had to finally acquiesce to their request.

Therefore, one evening, Gotama noticed that a frail cow had entered his hermitage and was eating the plants of his garden. He plucked a tiny twig and tried to shoo away the cow, but to his utter shock, the cow fell down dead. Word spread fast, and the rishis gathered around the dead cow. 'You have committed gohatya (killing of a cow)! And you claim to be a sage of the highest order!' a voice said. Another voice piped up, 'We never expected such actions from you. How could you do this?' Yet another said, 'What was the crime of this poor innocent cow that you have beaten it to death? It was your mistake to have kept the garden gate open.' Horrified, Gotama opened his mouth to protest his innocence but when he glanced at the rishis, he could feel their invisible darts of dislike and vengeance. He realized the futility of explaining but he wondered about the reasons behind their strange behaviour. He stood silently without a word of protest.

Ahalya, who had heard the commotion and rushed to her

husband's side, started to argue, but Gotama placed a hand on her shoulder and shook his head. Ahalya became silent.

One of them took over the mantle of leadership and addressed him, 'Gotama, you must leave this place immediately. We shall not tolerate such actions. Go away with your family and never show your faces again. You must never return to Brahmagiri.' Gotama could not believe his ears. He pleaded, 'I am ready to perform penance to expiate this sin. I know it was an unforgivable action but please believe me, it was not intentional. Please do not ask us to leave Brahmagiri. It has been our home since long and we have nowhere to go.' His pleas fell on deaf ears.

Thus, the family had to pack their few belongings and got ready to leave the place. Before leaving, Gotama approached the other rishis again and offered to atone for the sin. Finally, they became so exasperated with his pleas that they decided to pronounce near impossible conditions for him to fulfil. One of them said, 'You must first bathe in the Ganga and purify yourself. Then you should make one crore lingas of mud and perform abhisheka with hundreds of pots of Ganga water for each. Finally, you must perform circumambulation of the Brahmagiri hill 108 times. If you do this, then we shall consider that you have atoned for your sin. Now go away and leave us in peace.' As Gotama and his family walked away, they laughed and made fun of him among themselves.

Gotama was no ordinary rishi. He prayed intensely to Lord Siva who appeared before him and asked him what he desired. When Gotama wanted to be purified of the sin of gohatya, Siva revealed the truth behind the happenings. He said, 'Sage Gotama, you are spotless. You have not sinned. Ganesa had come in the form of an old cow on the insistence of your neighbours. So you have not killed a cow in reality.'

But Gotama insisted, 'O Great God, yet the world believes I have committed the sin of gohatya. Please let Gangaa flow here at Brahmagiri. I will bathe in her and also fulfil the other conditions laid down, with the help of the waters of Ganga. My fellow mates would not be able to do anything but accept me back into their fold. Also, all humanity can benefit from her pure waters.'

Hearing this, by the grace of Lord Siva, Gangaa appeared and bowing to Lord Siva said, 'My lord, I am willing to come down to earth but do not want to be separated from you. Please stay here with me for the sake of all your devotees.' She then took the form of water and began to flow through the branch of a fig tree as a river, just as desired by Sage Gotama. Lord Siva looked benignly at him. 'Are you satisfied now? I will bless this kshetra (region) as Tryambakesvara and Gangaa's waters will be known as Gautami here.'

After Lord Siva left, Sage Gotama, along with Ahalya and his pupils, worked on fulfilling the other conditions set for atonement. Despite becoming aware of the rishis' misdeeds, Gotama, like his *ishta-devataa* (chosen deity) Lord Siva, was unperturbed. He not only forgave all the rishis and their wives but also joyfully returned to his hermitage among them. Sage Gotama felt that the other rishis had done him a favour as they became the cause for him to behold Lord

Siva's divine self. Thus, the place became sanctified by Lord Siva's presence.

GOTAMA AND HIS STUDENT UTTANKA

Uttanka was Sage Gotama's favourite disciple and continued to stay in the gurukula long after he finished his studies. It was customary for a student to complete his studies and then take leave with the Guru's consent after giving *gurudakshinaa* (fees given to one's preceptor). Though all his other disciples left as they had come, Gotama never told Uttanka that he could return home. Uttanka patiently awaited his guru's directive.

One day, Uttanka went to the forest to fetch firewood. He took a long time to return and, when he did, he was so fatigued that as soon as he reached the hermitage, he collapsed to the ground. He was taken inside and water was sprinkled on his face. When he opened his eyes, Sage Gotama offered him water to drink and asked, 'Uttanka! What is the matter? Why did it take so long for you to return from the forest? Why are you so tired that you collapsed on reaching? What is it that ails you?'

Uttanka got up and placing his palms on his guru's feet begged for forgiveness saying, 'I have grown old and weak. It has been a 100 years since I came here for my education. I have served you and learned the scriptures from you. All my fellow mates have long since left the hermitage, I have not returned home though. Pray tell me, what have I done that you do not give me leave. This sorrow is aging me and I feel weak and ill. Forgive me.'

Sage Gotama was filled with remorse for not realizing his disciple's mind and for having kept him in the hermitage without paying heed to his aspirations. Sage Gotama lifted Uttanka by holding his shoulders and embraced him. 'My dearest Uttanka! You have learned all that I could teach you. You are free to leave and return to your people. I shall greatly miss you.'

Uttanka was instantly rejuvenated and smilingly said, 'Great Guru! I thank you with all my heart for your permission. Please grant another wish of mine. Kindly tell me what I should offer as gurudakshinaa. After that last task, I shall leave.'

Despite Sage Gotama's assurances that no gurudakshinaa was expected of him, Uttanka insisted until Sage Gotama sent him to Ahalya. She asked him to bring the divine earrings of Madayanti, wife of King Mitrasaha for her use.

King Mitrasaha, who had been turned into a rakshasa by the curse of Sage Vasishtha, was wandering in the forests. After a long journey, Uttanka reached the outskirts of the kingdom and approached King Mitrasaha, or Kalmashapada as he was now known, fearlessly. The rakshasa was about to pounce upon him and devour him when Uttanka introduced himself as Sage Gotama's student and put forth his request. The rakshasa was ravenous and not willing to spare him. But Uttanka promised to return to him after giving the earrings to Gotama's wife Ahalya.

Kalmashapada permitted him to meet his wife Madayanti and secure the earrings. Madayanti handed over her earrings amicably and warned him, 'Be careful, these earrings are divine and, therefore, coveted by many who may attempt to steal them from you. Do not place them on the ground.' Uttanka tied them in a deerskin and started on his return journey, happy to have achieved his goal. However, when he stopped to eat some fruit, the deerskin became untied and the earrings fell on the ground.

Takshaka, the king of serpents, who was also desirous of obtaining the earrings, was following Uttanka. As soon as the earrings fell to the ground, he grabbed them and slithered down an anthill. Uttanka began to dig the anthill with a stick, and continued thus for many days.

Indra, who happened to pass that way, took pity on him and hurled his vajra (Indra's weapon, the thunderbolt) on the anthill, opening up the way to Nagaloka. Uttanka pleaded with Takshaka to return the earrings but in vain. This time, Agni came to his rescue as a horse and emitted flames from all parts of his body, thus filling Nagaloka with fire and smoke. Takshaka emerged, begged for pardon and handed over the earrings.

Uttanka took the earrings and returned to Kalmashapada to inform him of his success and to assure him that he would return as his meal once he handed over the earrings to Ahalya. Kalmashapada was pleased with his steadfastness and truthfulness. He said, 'I do not wish to eat you anymore. There is no need to come back to me. Please go to your guru's asrama, hand over the earrings and live in peace.'

Uttanka reached his guru's asrama and gave the earrings to Ahalya. She was very pleased with the gurudakshinaa and approaching Sage Gotama said, 'Uttanka has passed the final test too. His gurudakshinaa is a real treasure.' She added, 'Our daughter is grown up and we need a suitable groom for her.' Sage Gotama replied, 'That would be a very good decision. However, it is against the Sastras for a student to marry his teacher's daughter. Also, due to his austerities and the power he has gained, no ordinary woman can become the wife of Uttanka. So I shall give our daughter a new body with the help of my spiritual powers. In this manner, she would become a different person and can marry Uttanka.'

With his spiritual powers, Sage Gotama turned Uttanka into a healthy and radiant youth. Sage Gotama and Ahalya performed the marriage of their daughter with Uttanka. He then built his own hermitage and lived there teaching students who came to him for learning Vedas and Sastras.

8

The Seven Sages

SAPTARSHIS' ROLE IN THE UNION OF SIVA AND PARVATI

After the death of Sati, Siva retreated from the world. His meditation was so severe that none dared approach him. In the meantime, Lord Brahma granted the asura, Taraka, the boon that he would die at the hands of Siva's son. Immediately, Taraka assumed he was immortal and attacked Devaloka. The Devas surrendered all their cherished treasures—Indra's mount Airaavata, the wish-yielding cow, Kaamadhenu, the celestial horse, Uccaisravas and the celestial wish-fulfilling tree, Kalpavriksha—without an iota of protest. Taraka then took control of the earth and other worlds without any opposition. He became the lord of the three worlds and his men caused havoc and carnage everywhere. The Devas and the mortals had no option but to endure.

Sati was reborn as Parvati, the daughter of Himavan and Menaka. When the tyranny of Taraka became unbearable, Devas sought refuge with Vishnu, who advised them to approach Siva. Terrified of the suggestion, the Devas implored Vishnu and Lord Brahma to accompany them. The Kinnaras, Caranas, Siddhas, Yakshas and Gandharvas joined the Devas, and all of them reached Kailasa. After much eulogizing, Siva opened his eyes and asked the reason for their visit.

Lord Brahma reminded the Trikaalajna—the knower of the past, present and future, another name for Siva—of the boon granted to Taraka, and begged him to marry Parvati. He said, 'Mahadeva, you know that Parvati is Sati, your Sakti reborn. Siva and Sakti are one. Parvati is performing rigorous tapas to obtain you as her husband. We all solicit you—nay, implore you—to accept her as your wife so that the son you beget from her will destroy Taraka and end the misery of us all.'

Siva looked thoughtful, and then spoke, 'I am not in the least inclined to become a householder again. But for the welfare of the world, I shall do as you request.' The Devas were thrilled and returned to their respective abodes with hope in their hearts.

Siva remembered the saptarshis, and they immediately appeared before him, their faces beaming with delight. 'Ocean of Mercy, we are indeed blessed that you have thought of us. Pray, how may we serve you?'

'Virtuous sages,' Siva said, 'The daughter of Himavan and Menaka is performing penance, desirous of obtaining me as her husband. You must test her steadfastness and resolve. Do not hesitate to make critical remarks against me if need be.' The saptarshis bowed and quickly went to the place where Parvati was performing austerities.

The mother of the universe warmly welcomed and worshipped them. She revealed her heart's desire for a union with Siva and added that she was doing penance at the bidding of Sage Narada. On hearing Narada's name, the saptarshis laughed aloud and said to Parvati, 'O wise and beautiful one, how did you allow yourself to be misled by that Narada? He professes to be a great scholar and a samaritan. But he is a mischief-monger. Have you not heard of how Narada misguided his own brothers?'

When Parvati gave a questioning look, they told her: 'Narada is the maanasaputra of Lord Brahma. He disobeyed his father who ordered him to marry and procreate, and chose to become a monk. Moreover, when Lord Brahma created the Sanatkumaras and instructed them likewise, it was Narada who advised them to engage in penance for the Parabrahman. The Sanatkumaras ended up bachelors like him! You, dear lady, have been fooled by him to indulge in such severe penance, all for the sake of Siva, who is indifferent to the world. And Siva's origin is unknown; he is homeless and a wanderer. He is so poor that he cannot feed himself. He married Sati, the daughter of Dakshaprajapati, but could he maintain her? Now, he is meditating on himself! Listen to us, daughter, and do as we bid you. Go home and marry someone suitable, your equal in beauty, wealth and knowledge.'

Parvati laughed and replied. 'I bow to your wisdom and conduct, great sages. but I cannot accept what you say. Sage Narada is my guru and his instructions are the Vedas to me. How does it matter if Siva is not wealthy or handsome or wise! He is compassion incarnate to his devotees, he is bliss personified, he is the Supreme One. Nothing you say can deter me from my resolve. If he does not marry me, I shall forever remain a virgin.' Parvati paid obeisance to the sages and returned to her penance.

The saptarshis were delighted and, returning to Kailasa, narrated all this to Siva and took his leave.

Thereafter, Siva himself took the form of an ordinary ascetic and approached Parvati in order to test her. After Parvati had welcomed and worshipped the ascetic, he asked her the reasons for her austerities. When Parvati answered that she had accepted Siva as her husband with *trikaranas* (thought, word and action), the ascetic made disparaging remarks about Siva. He said: 'That homeless wanderer! That naked beggar! His parentage is unknown. He has matted hair, wears snakes as ornaments, tiger or elephant skin if he decides to get dressed, smears his body with ash. What do you see in him that you desire him? His companions are ghosts and goblins. He does not have a single quality that is pleasing. O jewel among women, you and Siva are poles apart, give up this foolishness and return to your parents. They will find a suitable groom for you.'

Parvati blazed in fury, rebuked him and glorified the greatness of Siva. She then ordered the ascetic to leave the place at once. Siva manifested himself and clasped her hand. 'You have won me, my dear, I am now your slave.' Parvati blushed and bid Siva to ask her father for her hand in marriage.

Siva summoned the saptarshis again and instructed them to take his marriage proposal to Himavan and Menaka. The saptarshis were delighted to act as matchmakers. After they were worshipped by Himavan and Menaka and asked about the purpose of their visit, the sages spoke thus: 'Siva is the Father of the universe, and your daughter is the Mother. Her rightful place is beside Siva. By giving your consent to this alliance, your life will become fruitful.'

After some persuasion, the royal couple agreed. They entertained the sages with a grand feast, after which an auspicious day for the marriage was determined. When the saptarshis returned to Kailasa and apprised Siva, he beamed with pleasure. Then he expressed his ignorance about the wedding customs.

The sages were amused at the Lord's naiveté and said, 'Please summon Vishnu and Lord Brahma and hand over the responsibility of the wedding arrangements to them. They will suitably instruct the Devas led by Indra to take care of everything.'

The saptarshis returned later to Kailasa to attend the wedding. After the marriage of Siva and Parvati, a son named Kartikeya was born to them. He killed the demon Taraka in battle and brought peace to the world.

SAPTARSHIS WRITE THE RAMAYANA

The seven sages were jointly involved in certain activities and major events. They were the joint authors of a Ramayana called Saptarshi Ramayana, which has just seven verses. Each verse was composed by one of the sages and described the various events that took place in a kaanda. Thus, the verse for Balakanda was composed by Kasyapa, Ayodhyakanda by Atri, Aranyakanda by Bharadvaja, Kishkindhakanda by Visvamitra, Sundarakanda by Gotama, Yuddhakanda by Jamadagni and Uttarakanda by Vasishtha. An additional verse mentioning the merits of reciting these verses known as *phalasruti* (reward for reciters) was composed by all of them together. Saptarshi Ramayana and its meaning are as follows:

jaatah sriiraghunaayako dasarathaan munyaasrayaat taatakaam
hatvaa rakshita-kausika-kratu-varah krtvaapy ahalyaam subhaam |
bhanktvaa rudra-saraasanam janakajaam paanau grihiitvaa tato
jitvaa'rdhaa'dhvani bhaargavam punaragaat siitaa-sametah puriim || (i)

Sri Rama, born of Dasaratha, King of Ayodhya, followed Visvamitra to the forest, where he killed Tataka and protected the great yajna of Visvamitra. He then sanctified Ahalya, broke the bow of Siva and married Sita, the daughter of King Janaka of Videha. He defeated Parashurama and,

The Seven Sages

accompanied by Sita, returned to the city of Ayodhya.

*daasyaa mantharayaa dayaa-rahitayaa durbheditaa kaikayii
sriirama-prathamaabhisheka-samaye maataapy ayaacad varau |
bhartaaram bharatah prasaastu dharaniim raamo vanam gacchataad
ityaakarnya sa cottaram nahi dadau duhkhena muurchaam gatah ||* (ii)

Manthara, the ruthless slave, poisoned the pure mind of Kaikeyi who sought two boons from her husband at the time of the coronation of Rama—Bharata was to be crowned king and Rama to be exiled for 14 years. Hearing this, Dasaratha gave no answer but, experiencing great sorrow, fell unconscious.

*sriiraamah pitrisaasanaad vanam agaat saumitrisiitaanvito
gangaam praapya jataam nibadhya saguhah saccitrakuute vasan |
krtvaa tatra pitrkriyaam sabharato datvaabhayam dandake
praapyaagastyamuniisvaram taduditam dhrtvaa dhanuscaakshayam ||* (iii)

At his father's command, Rama went to the forest accompanied by Lakshmana and Sita. On reaching the Ganga, he matted his hair and stayed at the charming Citrakuta with Guha (The king of tribals of Sringaverapura and friend of Rama). He performed the obsequies, along with Bharata for his father, gave abhaya (assurance of safety) to the rishis and met Agastya, the lord of sages. And on request, he carried the bow along with the inexhaustible quiver of arrows.

gatvaa pancavatiim agastyavacanaad datvaabhayam mauninaam
chitvaa surpanakhaasyakarnayugalam traatum samastaan muniin |
hatvaa tam ca kharam suvarna harinam bhitvaa tathaa vaalinam
 taaraaratnam avairiraajyam akarot sarvam ca sugriivasaat || (iv)

As directed by Agastya, Rama went to Pancavati and gave abhaya to the sages there. Surpanakha's nose was chopped off, and to protect the sages, Rama killed Khara. Later, while he pursued the golden deer, Sita was abducted by Ravana. During his search for Sita, Rama killed Vali. He handed over Vali's wife, the beautiful Tara, and the kingdom to Sugriva.

duuto daasaratheh saliilam udadhim tiirtvaa hanuumaan mahaan
drishtvaa'sokavane sthitaam janakajaam datvaa'ngulermudrikaam |
akshaadiin asuraan nihatya mahatiim lankaam ca dagdhvaa punah
sriiraamam ca sametya deva jananii drishtaa mayetyabraviit || (v)

The Seven Sages

The great Hanuman, messenger of Sri Rama, crossed the ocean easily, met Sita in the Asoka Garden and gave her the signet ring. He killed demons such as Aksha and set fire to Lanka. Then he returned to Rama and narrated: 'Mother Sita was seen by me.'

raamo baddhapayonidhih kapivarair viirair nalaadyair vrito
lankaam praapya sa kumbhakarnatanujam hatvaa rane raavanam |
tasyaam nyasya vibhiishanam punarasau siitaapatih pushpakaa-
ruudhassan puram aagatas sabharatah simhaasanastho babhau || (vi)

Rama built a bridge across the ocean with the help of monkeys such as Nala and others and reached Lanka. He killed Ravana, Kumbhakarna and their sons. He then put Vibhisana on the throne and arrived at Ayodhya in the Pushpaka vimaana. He was coronated and ruled alongwith Bharata as prince.

sriiraamo hayamedha mukhya makhakrit samyak prajaah paalayan
kritvaa raajyam athaanujaisca suciram bhuuri svadharmaanvitau |
putrau bhraatrisutaanvitau kusalavau samsthaapya bhuumandale
 so'yodhyaapura- vaasibhisca sarayuusnaatah prapede divam || (vii)

After performing Asvamedha Yajna, Rama ruled the kingdom along with his brothers, looking after his subjects well. He installed Kusa and Lava, who were following *svadharma* (one's own duty) in the company of his brothers' sons. Then, along with the citizens of Ayodhya, Rama took a bath in the river Sarayu and returned to the heavens.

sriiramasyakathaa sudhaatimadhuraan slokaan imaan uttamaan
ye srinvanti pathanti ca pratidinam te'ghaugha vidhvamsinah |
sriimanto bahuputrapautrasahitaa bhuktveha bhogaamsciram
bhogaante tu sadaarcitam suraganair vishnor labhante padam || *(viii)*

The sins of those who listen to and read these sweet verses of Rama's story daily will be destroyed and they will be blessed with prosperity. For a long time, they will enjoy pleasures with their sons and grandsons. After enjoyment, they will attain the abode of Lord Vishnu, who is worshipped by the gods.

SAPTARSHIS TEACH KING VRSHADARBHI A LESSON

The saptarshis decided to travel around the world with the purpose of intensifying their austerities. At that time, the land was afflicted with such a severe drought that the sages had to forage for food. They barely survived on fruits and roots in the forests. The sages became so weak that they found it extremely difficult to even perform their nitya karmas.

One day, King Vrshadarbhi chanced upon the saptarshis and, seeing their pitiable condition, offered them cattle, lands, gold and grains as gifts. 'Great sages, why do you roam these forests in search of food? Why do you suffer so, pray tell me?' When he received no reply, he continued: 'All of you have the wealth of tapas, but let me tell what wealth I have. I can give you the food you seek. Ascetics who seek gifts from me are very dear to me. If only you ask, I shall provide each of you a 1,000 cows, each having a newly-born calf and, therefore, providing milk. I shall also gift each of you a 1,000 bulls, strong and well-proportioned. I shall grant a 100 villages each and give you enough grain for a whole year. Do not punish yourselves thus, just tell me what you want from me.'

The saptarshis replied. 'O King, accepting gifts from a monarch is most inappropriate for ascetics. By acceptance of gifts we shall lose the merit that we have acquired. Why do you tempt us so? Even though we do not accept your gifts we bless you with prosperity.'

Sage Atri said, 'All the land and wealth of the world cannot satisfy a man. Hence, one who seeks true happiness should learn contentment.'

Visvamitra said, 'When one desire is fulfilled, another will arise, and then another, and so on. Where is the end?'

The other sages too expressed similar views. The saptarshis then continued on their way. King Vrshadarbhi was furious at being snubbed. He was the son of the famous King Sibi, renowned for his magnanimity and sacrifice. But he was the exact opposite of his father in character and, hence, the sages rejected his charity.

During their wanderings, a mendicant by name Sunassakha and his dog joined the group. 'Great sages, please allow me to accompany you as you travel through these forests. It is my good fortune that I behold you all together, how many people are blessed with such an opportunity? Let me gain from your discourses and discussions.' Though the saptarshis found the request strange, they agreed. Thus, the sages continued, trying to keep their minds focused only on austerities, but also concerned about the sustenance of their bodies.

In the meantime, King Vrshadarbhi was determined to avenge himself and performed a special yajna. From the flames of the sacrificial fire arose a rakshasi named Yatudhani. King Vrshadarbhi ordered her to destroy the saptarshis. The rakshasi reached the area where the sages were and stood guard near a lake filled with lotuses. When the sages neared the lake, they noticed that she was standing by and asked her permission to enter the lake. Yatudhani agreed to allow them to enter the water only if each sage explained the meaning of their respective names. The saptarshis gave the meaning of their names and entered the lake.

But when it was Sage Sunassakha's turn, he said, 'I am

Sage Sunassakha. I am not willing to explain the meaning of my name to you. I am declaring that I am Sage Sunassakha, you must be satisfied with it.' Yatudhani was furious and repeated her condition. Sage Sunassakha struck her with his danda and she fell down dead. As the saptarshis looked on in astonishment, Sage Sunassakha transformed himself into Indra and stood before them.

Indra bowed to the saptarshis and said, 'I knew of King Vrshadarbhi's evil intentions when he performed the yajna. He wanted to kill you and, hence, sent Yatudhani. I did not want you to lose the tapas sakti that you are trying to gain. Also, it is my duty to protect you. Hence, I joined you as Sage Sunassakha. Pray grant me leave and I shall return to Devaloka.' Indra vanished and the saptarshis completed their journey.

Acknowledgements

I would like to express my gratitude to my sister for her valuable inputs in researching material for *Saptarshis*, to my father who in my eyes is the greatest authority on mythology, to my mother who encouraged me to write and my brother for allowing me to work undisturbed.

I am grateful to Rupa Publications for publishing this work, Sakschi Verma for keeping her patience with my idiosyncrasies and to Nishtha Kapil who oversaw the entire project and kept the flock together. Without the coordination of every person in the Rupa team, completion of this book would not have been possible.

Last but not the least, I am thankful to my readers who I hope will enjoy reading this book as much as I enjoyed writing it!